Motivated to
Learn

Decreasing Challenging Student Behaviors & Increasing Academic Engagement

Staci M. Zolkoski • Calli Lewis Chiu • Mandy E. Lusk

Solution Tree | Press a division of
Solution Tree

555 North Morton Street
Bloomington, IN 47404
800.733.6786 (toll free) / 812.336.7700
FAX: 812.336.7790

email: info@SolutionTree.com
SolutionTree.com

Visit **go.SolutionTree.com/behavior** to download the free reproducibles in this book.

Printed in the United States of America

Library of Congress Cataloging-in-Publication Data

Names: Zolkoski, Staci M., author. | Chiu, Calli Lewis, author. | Lusk, Mandy E., author.
Title: Motivated to learn : decreasing challenging student behaviors and increasing academic engagement / Staci M. Zolkoski, Calli Lewis Chiu, Mandy E. Lusk.
Description: Bloomington, IN : Solution Tree Press, [2022] | Includes bibliographical references and index.
Identifiers: LCCN 2022015754 (print) | LCCN 2022015755 (ebook) | ISBN 9781952812835 (Paperback) | ISBN 9781952812842 (eBook)
Subjects: LCSH: Classroom management--United States. | Behavior modification--United States. | Motivation in education--United States. | Teacher-student relationships--United States. | Education--Research--United States.
Classification: LCC LB3013 .Z65 2022 (print) | LCC LB3013 (ebook) | DDC 371.102/4--dc23/eng/20220713
LC record available at https://lccn.loc.gov/2022015754
LC ebook record available at https://lccn.loc.gov/2022015755

Solution Tree
Jeffrey C. Jones, CEO
Edmund M. Ackerman, President

Solution Tree Press
President and Publisher: Douglas M. Rife
Associate Publisher: Sarah Payne-Mills
Managing Production Editor: Kendra Slayton
Editorial Director: Todd Brakke
Art Director: Rian Anderson
Copy Chief: Jessi Finn
Production Editor: Kate St. Ives
Content Development Specialist: Amy Rubenstein
Acquisitions Editor: Sarah Jubar
Copy Editor: Jessi Finn
Proofreader: Elisabeth Abrams
Cover Designer: Abigail Bowen
Text Designer: Julie Csizmadia
Associate Editor: Sarah Ludwig
Editorial Assistants: Charlotte Jones and Elijah Oates

We dedicate this book to Dr. Lyndal M. Bullock.
His leadership and advocacy for students
with emotional and behavior disorders
continually inspire our teaching.

Acknowledgments

We thank Sean, Colton, Zoe, Allen, Sara, Keith, Ella, and all our family, friends, and mentors who have encouraged us and have been our champions along the way.

We thank Sarah for being the best editor to work with.

We also thank our former students, who helped us become the best teachers we could be and showed us how much we love working with kids.

And to all the practicing and future teachers who are reading this book, we wrote it for you!

Solution Tree Press would like to thank the following reviewers:

Taylor Bronowicz
Math Teacher
Sparkman Middle School
Toney, Alabama

Molly Capps
Principal
McDeeds Creek Elementary
Southern Pines, North Carolina

Charlcy Carpenter
Math Teacher
Burns Middle School
Lawndale, North Carolina

Jen Didech
Math Teacher
Twin Groves Middle School
Buffalo Grove, Illinois

Charles Ames Fischer
Educational Consultant
Decatur, Tennessee

Kelli Fuller
Instructional Facilitator
Howard Perrin Elementary School
Benton, Arkansas

Cheryl Hermach
Language Arts Teacher
Lafayette High School
Wildwood, Missouri

Kelly Hilliard
Math Teacher
McQueen High School
Reno, Nevada

Nancy J. Petolick
Instructional Coach
Sandbrock Ranch Elementary
Aubrey, Texas

Dawn Vang
Assistant Principal
McDeeds Creek Elementary
Southern Pines, North Carolina

Lindi Wilson
Curriculum Instructor
Barrett Elementary School
Birmingham, Alabama

Visit **go.SolutionTree.com/behavior** to download
the free reproducibles in this book.

Table of Contents

Reproducibles are in italics.

About the Authors

 **Staci M. Zolkoski, PhD,** is an associate professor of special education at the University of Texas at Tyler (UT Tyler). Prior to working at the collegiate level, Dr. Zolkoski taught kindergarten and fourth grade. She teaches classroom management at the undergraduate and graduate levels as well as courses in special education, behavior disorders, and educational strategies. She has won the Kappa Delta Pi International Honor Society Teacher of the Year award for the UT Tyler School of Education two times and for the UT Tyler College of Education and Psychology one time.

Dr. Zolkoski is a member of the Council for Exceptional Children as well as an active member of the Division for Emotional and Behavioral Health (DEBH), where she serves on the publications and professional development committees. She is the treasurer of the DEBH Foundation and the editor of the DEBH newsletter, *Behavior Today*. Dr. Zolkoski has presented and published her research on resilience and social-emotional learning at the national and international levels. She has worked with local school districts to implement social-emotional learning and has trained teachers and schools in social-emotional learning and classroom management. Dr. Zolkoski has also presented for ElevateTXEd, which is a collaborative effort across the University of Texas System.

Dr. Zolkoski earned her bachelor's degree in early childhood education from the University of Toledo in Ohio. She earned her master's degree and doctorate in special education with an emphasis on behavior disorders from the University of North Texas.

Calli Lewis Chiu, PhD, is an associate professor in the Department of Special Education at California State University, Fullerton (CSUF). Before joining CSUF in 2018, she was an assistant professor at California State University, Bakersfield and Shippensburg University. Prior to entering academia, Dr. Lewis Chiu was a special education teacher for ten years and worked as a direct care service provider for adolescents in foster care. Her teaching expertise is instruction for children and youth with emotional and behavioral disorders. She has numerous publications and presentations related to improving outcomes for students with emotional and behavioral disorders and increasing cultural competence among preservice teachers.

Dr. Lewis Chiu holds a bachelor of fine arts in art education from Texas Tech University, a master of education with an emphasis on multicultural issues in special education from the University of Texas at Austin, and a doctorate with an emphasis on emotional and behavioral disorders in special education from the University of North Texas.

Mandy E. Lusk, PhD, is a lifelong special educator who serves as an associate professor of special education at Clayton State University. As a special education practitioner for numerous years, Dr. Lusk predominantly taught students of all ages with emotional and behavioral disorders across the United States. She worked at Wichita State University and then started a special education certification program at Clayton State University. Dr. Lusk's research agenda includes preparing teachers to effectively educate diverse learners with challenging behaviors.

Dr. Lusk earned her undergraduate degree in special education and master's degree in students with behavior disorders from Mississippi State University. She earned a doctorate focused on students with behavior disorders from the University of North Texas.

To book Staci M. Zolkoski, Calli Lewis Chiu, or Mandy E. Lusk for professional development, contact pd@SolutionTree.com.

Introduction

"Jarrod is a seventh grader—I don't know what to do about him! He is all over the place. He touches other students' stuff and disrupts their concentration. He refuses to finish his classwork and hinders others from finishing theirs."

"When I tell Sasha, an eleventh grader, what class assignment to do, I'm ignored. When I repeat myself, I'm ignored again. So, I repeat myself yet again and tell her that if she doesn't answer, I'm sending her to the office. She gets up and leaves. I want compliance."

"Derek, a second grader, will begin his independent mathematics assignment, but he often wants me to sit with him to complete it. He is capable of completing the work on his own; however, he lacks the motivation to finish it independently."

We (Staci, Calli, and Mandy) are aware that many of you, as teachers, can relate to these student scenarios. We understand that students with challenging behaviors can negatively alter your school day and perhaps even your outlook on teaching. Each of us has been in that place of discouragement. We've spent long nights reviewing the cumulative folders of students who display problematic behaviors, trying to find the *solution* to their issues. We have tried sympathizing with these students one week and taking a sterner approach the next. We have exhausted ourselves searching on our computers for research findings and strategies that we can immediately implement for these students, knowing that a basic internet search is unlikely to give us the professional or research-based answers we need.

The following snapshots come from our experiences as teachers struggling and eventually—through learning, developing, and implementing new strategies— succeeding in addressing challenging behaviors students have brought to our classrooms.

Staci reflects:

> My teacher-preparation program included a few courses in special education but no courses in classroom management. Although I was a general education kindergarten and fourth-grade teacher, each year, I had several students with disabilities as well as some very active students who some would call the "problem students." I found that I loved working with these students because I could tell they were good kids but misunderstood. Providing them a little bit of encouragement and being their champion made their faces light up, and they began to talk to me more. I could tell I was making a difference even though I wasn't really doing much but showing them I cared about them and their education. This was something, but I wanted to do more. I constantly looked for strategies to help my students be successful. I went back to school to get my master's degree in special education with an emphasis on behavior disorders.
>
> As I was finishing my degree, I moved from kindergarten to fourth grade, and that's when I met a student named Cody. I got an earful of negative information from his previous teacher but did not let it scare me away. He was a tough student. He had built walls from his years of adverse experiences and often came across as defensive. His parents, particularly his mom, were abrasive.
>
> I was excited to put my training to use, thinking I was magically going to make his school experience better overnight, and boy, did he prove me wrong! Through persistence, I began to develop positive relationships with Cody and his parents by getting to know all of them; I even went to his football games. Changing years of negative experiences takes time, even with the best strategies in place. The road was often bumpy, but Cody and his family knew I cared about him and wanted him to be successful. Years later, I got a message from Cody and his mom telling me that being in my classroom had changed his schooling experience and helped him continue on even though he still did not always have the best school experiences after leaving my class. He is currently in the U.S. Army Infantry.

Calli recalls:

I didn't have a single classroom-management or behavior-management course in my teacher-preparation program. Needless to say, I entered my first year of teaching completely unprepared to navigate students' challenging behaviors. I remember asking my colleagues for advice and being told more than once to put some type of reward system in place. I remember thinking, *Nope! The students should know how to behave.* I struggled for a couple of years and then started paying attention to what was happening in classes that flowed smoothly, and I finally started implementing the strategies you'll find in this book. There was a lot of trial and error, but I got it! In my last year of teaching before I left to pursue my PhD, my middle schoolers were working on a draft of their essay when my assistant principal opened my classroom door, stuck his head inside, and whispered to me, "Oh, sorry! I didn't know they were testing!" I replied, "They aren't. They're just all on task!"

And Mandy remembers:

Several years into teaching, I met Virgie. I thought I was well prepared, or even overprepared, for a student like Virgie. After all, I had earned two degrees in special education (a bachelor's degree in special education and a master's degree in behavior disorders). I was wrong. Virgie, a sixth-grade student, lived with his single mother, his younger sister, and his mom's continuously shifting social circle and unstable relationships, which disrupted his home environment. His eyes revealed his anger for life and disdain for school. I took his anger personally more times than I care to admit. His apathy seemed directed specifically at me. I often wondered if taking directives from a female teacher was difficult for him due to his troubled relationship with his mother. He didn't seem to respond the same way to male paraprofessionals in our classroom.

I could count at least five tier 1 and tier 2 positive behavior interventions and supports (PBIS) practices implemented within our classroom that were structured for student success. I perceived that the other students in my classroom responded positively to these tiered strategies; however, Virgie did not. He would sit at his desk, shout profanities, taunt his peers, and refuse to work. I asked myself hundreds of times a day, "How can these interventions not work?" The situation seemed hopeless. After working with me for two years, Virgie finally made strides with one of the evidence-based practices that we will be discussing in this book.

After twenty-plus years each of teaching in classrooms, and after years of training to work with individuals who behave in challenging ways, we know how difficult it is to motivate and engage students who exhibit resistant and even hostile behaviors. And we know how difficult it is to learn how to address these behaviors through a slow and sometimes confusing process of trial and error. It's even more frustrating when you lack adequate strategies to bring positive change to this difficult work. These are the reasons why we wrote this book for you, novice and veteran K–12 teachers. Through practical, evidence-based, culturally responsive, and easy-to-implement strategies, we provide you the tools you need to address the challenging behaviors in your classroom so that you can spend your energy developing engaging lessons and building positive relationships with *all* your students. While you may have heard of the strategies in this book's eight chapters, or you may be familiar with some of them, we provide specific guidance to make sure you understand how to implement each strategy with fidelity and guarantee the best outcomes for you and your students.

Chapter 1 begins with an examination of factors that can contribute to challenging behaviors in students. We look at environmental factors stemming from aspects of students' nurturing, such as their family, community, teachers, and peers, and we look at the role genetic predisposition might play. Next, we consider unproductive reactions to challenging behaviors; these reactions of both the students themselves and the adults in the students' lives include developing learned helplessness and ascribing blame for students' challenging behaviors rather than addressing the behaviors. We then pair this consideration of unproductive reactions with productive behaviors and mindsets that help lay a foundation for effectively implementing the seven evidence-based strategies that make up the core of this book.

Chapters 2–8 encompass the seven strategies themselves: (1) student choice, (2) token economies, (3) high-probability sequencing, (4) classwide peer tutoring, (5) self-monitoring, (6) opportunities to respond, and (7) precorrection. Each chapter provides detailed guidance on the strategy it addresses, ideas for reinforcing the strategy, culturally responsive practices related to the strategy, tips for incorporating student interests into strategy implementation, and problem-solving tips for the strategy. A fictional scenario based on real-life school and student situations is also woven throughout each chapter to illuminate the issues and strategy the chapter addresses. Chapters close with a Concluding Thoughts section and a "Questions for Reflection" reproducible that invites readers to write in the spaces provided and in doing so envision themselves implementing the chapter's strategies, confronting challenges, exploring benefits, and so on. This book includes additional reproducible templates of helpful figures and an appendix of print and online resources that are linked to each chapter's content.

We offer this book as a comprehensive resource for any educator looking for guidance on working with students who have challenging behaviors. It will give you a wealth of tools and the flexibility of a toolbox, wherein you may move about the chapters in the order that works for you, choosing the strategies that fit your needs. When you finish reading, you will be able to motivate all students to engage in academic work.

Chapter 1

Why Students Exhibit Challenging Behaviors and How These Behaviors Impact Academic Engagement

Myra is a fourth grader who enjoys reading tween comedic books and playing with her friends. She is kind and calm. She is in the gifted program at school. Her brother, George, is a third grader at the same school who enjoys anything related to sports and mathematics. He is vivacious, assertive, and hysterical. He is currently in special education for specific learning disabilities in reading and challenging behaviors. Myra has many friends at school. George struggles with interpersonal skills, so he is unable to sustain friendships. He often tags along with Myra to social events at school. The two siblings are inseparable. Even though they are being raised in the same home environment by two supportive and consistent parental figures—(1) their single mom and (2) their maternal grandmother—they respond to authority very differently. George often displays challenging behaviors, yelling at his peers and teachers and clenching his fists when he is given directives that he doesn't like.

Think about your current and past students. Have you ever had a student exhibit behaviors like George's? What behaviors in your classroom are most frustrating for you? What problematic behaviors do you find yourself addressing over and over with your students? These behaviors may include being physically or verbally aggressive, bullying others, leaving a designated area, damaging property, being tardy to class, or throwing tantrums, to name a few. *Challenging behaviors* are defined as behaviors that are culturally or socially inappropriate (Emerson, 1995). Teachers need to address these behaviors because they can have an array of adverse consequences. Typically, in the classroom, behaviors are considered challenging when they prevent the student and his, her, or their peers from learning academically and socially (Scott, 2017).

Identifying the factors that may be contributing to students' challenging behaviors can lead you to develop effective intervention and prevention strategies for the students. So it is helpful to think about *why* students behave in these challenging ways.

Many factors can directly or indirectly influence student behaviors. This chapter begins by looking at various causal factors, which can be divided into two broad categories: (1) nurture and (2) nature. While no conclusive evidence indicates one factor is directly responsible for challenging behaviors (Hallahan, Kauffman, & Pullen, 2019; Yell, Meadows, Drasgow, & Shriner, 2013), a student like George from the opening scenario may be predisposed to exhibit problematic behaviors based on some factors, and other factors may trigger the behaviors in him. Meanwhile, Myra, for instance, does not experience this. The chapter then examines the relationship between challenging behaviors and academic achievement. Next, it delves into common obstacles teachers may face in approaching challenging behaviors and effective approaches teachers can use to counter these obstacles. The chapter also sets the foundation for the strategies in the book by articulating how preventive measures, positive behavior interventions and supports (PBIS), and cultural responsiveness undergird each of the following strategies. Last, this chapter wraps up with a Concluding Thoughts section and a reproducible page that includes reflective questions to ponder. The chapter will revisit the George and Myra scenario throughout to make the concepts of the chapter visible within an imaginary school context.

NURTURE

Nurture pertains to environmental influences and how they affect the way a person acts (Stiles, 2011). People's environment, upbringing, and life experiences condition them to act a specific way. In other words, people can learn behavior, and the environmental factors that affect an individual contribute to how adaptive or maladaptive that individual's behaviors are, particularly within a social context like school. Four primary sources of importance can offer or withhold the nurturing care that may be critical for a student to successfully function both within school and throughout life. These sources are (1) family, (2) community, (3) teachers and schools, and (4) peers and peer groups.

Family

The principal characters of the film *Lilo & Stitch* state simply, "*Ohana* means family. *Family* means nobody gets left behind or forgotten" (Sanders & DeBlois, 2002). In a perfect world, *all* students' families would be safe havens focused on the welfare of children. But research shows how parenting varies considerably and parenting behaviors contribute as protective or risk factors for behavior problems (White & Renk, 2012).

According to education researchers and authors James M. Kauffman and Timothy J. Landrum (2018), the following are the primary functions of *any* family with children.

- Protect children and provide care.

- Regulate children's behavior.

- Pass on essential knowledge and skills for understanding and navigating the physical and social world.

- Help shape and guide interactions and relationships.

- Facilitate children's understanding of themselves.

In reality, parents' supportiveness ranges from rejecting and unresponsive to warm and responsive. When families exhibit a lack of support and nurturing characteristics, their children *may* demonstrate challenging behaviors. Specifically, low supportiveness from parents is associated with poor psychological (for example, mental and emotional) outcomes that start in childhood and may continue to impact children later in their lives (Brumariu & Kerns, 2010).

Children living in adverse conditions (for example, physical or emotional neglect) in early childhood (birth to fifty-four months) will enter school at a disadvantage that leads to a greater possibility of school failure later in their lives. This is especially true for children who experience multiple risk factors over a long period of time (Sektnan, McClelland, Acock, & Morrison, 2010). Individuals in the family may also increase a child's chances of developing challenging behaviors if these family members are dealing with family conflict, are navigating a family history of mental illness, are neglectful or abusive, are harsh and inconsistent with discipline, or are struggling with addiction (Hallahan et al., 2019).

Let's imagine that instead of being a source of consistent support, as she is in the scenario that opens this chapter, Myra and George's mom battles debilitating chronic depression. Her mother, the siblings' grandmother, lives with the family to help when the mom is unable to provide the care that the children need (that is, help with regularly served, nutritious meals; help getting ready for school; and help with homework after school). Myra and George live within an environment that offers love and, in many ways, consistency and support. But the depression that their mother struggles with represents a stressor and is a likely factor—though not the only one—contributing to George's challenging behaviors. While this imagined addition to the introductory scenario makes explicit the ways a parent may not be available to meet physical needs, the parent may also not be available emotionally. Emotional unavailability can lead to perceived rejection, internalizing behaviors (for example, anxiety), and externalizing behaviors (for example, aggression) in children and adolescents. Parents who lack warmth or who display overprotection may also promote children's risk for internalizing and externalizing behavior challenges (White & Renk, 2012).

Parents and other family members have the capability to promote prosocial behaviors that protect against risk factors for children's challenging behaviors (White & Renk, 2012). Nurturing and supportive parents, family stability, and consistent discipline are factors that can lower risk and foster prosocial behaviors (Hallahan et al., 2019).

Educators are on the front lines interacting with students and the dynamics of their families daily. When it comes to challenging behaviors in students, don't forget the importance of supporting families (Hallahan et al., 2019). The National Federation of Families (www.ffcmh.org) has a fantastic website full of resources to support families. Most parents of children who have challenging behaviors, like George, want them to act more appropriately and will do anything to help them be successful. Rather than criticizing or blaming parents, educators need to act from a place of empathy and support. Parents need teachers to listen to them with an open mind. When parents and teachers work together, students are more successful.

Community

When you think about students, it helps to consider the community in which you teach. Is there plenty of green space? Do people have easy access to grocery stores? Is the community safe? Maybe the community in which you teach is the opposite of those ideals—a densely packed population, a concentrated number of fast-food restaurants and convenience stores with little fresh produce, and high levels of crime. The effects of class discrimination directly impact students in ways that manifest in their school performance (Gorski, 2018).

Consider green space, for example, which is often plentiful in wealthy neighborhoods. Research consistently supports that students who have access to nature have lower stress levels, fewer challenging behaviors, reduced symptoms of attention deficit disorder (ADD), and higher standardized test scores than students who have limited access to nature (McCormick, 2017).

Students who grow up in neighborhoods with limited resources face overwhelming challenges that their peers in affluent neighborhoods do not encounter (Jensen, 2009). Communities where students are regularly exposed to threats to their health and safety and to chronic and acute stress can serve as obstacles to strong school performance. In communities with low financial resources, there is often a higher prevalence of inadequate housing, poor health care, depression, and teen motherhood. In his book *Teaching With Poverty in Mind*, author and educator Eric Jensen (2009) says families that experience these factors can demonstrate a decreased capacity for sensitivity toward infants and young children, which can in turn manifest as poor academic performance and challenging behavior in students.

Consider this high-stakes factor that more commonly occurs in lower-socioeconomic-status (lower-SES) neighborhoods than in affluent areas: violence. Research supports that direct and indirect exposure to violence distresses students, negatively impacts their mental health and academic performance, and can lead to anxiety and aggression (Ozer, Lavi, Douglas, & Wolf, 2017). Regarding the relationship between what happens in a school and what happens in the surrounding community, violence in neighborhoods can have ripple effects among students (Burdick-Will, 2018). When students live with high levels of neighborhood violence, the schools can experience more disciplinary problems, students and teachers can feel less safe, and according to sociology and education researcher Julia Burdick-Will (2018), students have reported feeling less trust in their teachers.

Children and youth can display anxiety and aggression when they feel hypervigilant about perceived threats, and this hypervigilance can become a child's default state when living with neighborhood violence. Students who live in a neighborhood where violence is a regular occurrence may incorrectly interpret others' actions as hostile due to unconscious responses to fear and stress. Burdick-Will (2018) finds that adolescents who experience neighborhood violence may resort to using aggression to keep others in their neighborhood from bothering them.

Students who are reacting to their environments may not be inclined to engage in violent behavior, yet their peers, classmates, and teachers could misinterpret their actions. A cycle of misunderstanding can develop in which those in the classroom feel less safe and relationships between students and teachers deteriorate.

To reverse the complicated dynamics that can evolve between teachers and students of different socioeconomic statuses, teachers must focus not on the student as the problem but on their own practices as catalysts to support students. Teachers can support their students by drawing on their strengths and meeting them where they are (Gorski, 2018). Likewise, it is crucial that teachers conceptualize neighborhoods with large numbers of families living below the poverty line as more than collections of poor people (Milner, Cunningham, Murray, & Alvarez, 2017). Teachers should observe the ways in which students navigate and persist despite obstacles associated with poverty and learn about various supports they receive from their families and communities.

Let's revisit the scenario involving George and Myra.

George and Myra have a loving and supportive mother and grandmother. This is very clear to George's teacher, Mr. Riley. George's mother always calls to confirm George's assignments even when she can't make it to parent-teacher conferences due to her minimum-income job that does not include paid time off—or time off period! George's grandmother often drops by with a box of doughnuts she got from the discount shelf at her local supermarket, a gift for George's class to share. While George's mother's efforts are commendable, Mr. Riley can't help but feel that they are a bit futile and that, no matter what, she's just going to be a bit more out of touch with George's school life than if her circumstances allowed her to be more present at the school. Mr. Riley also recognizes that George's grandmother's gesture is incredibly kind and supportive. Even so, he typically throws the doughnuts away without offering them as a snack to students. High-sugar foods aren't good, right? And the yellow discount tag deters him—what if the doughnuts are expired?

"They do what they can," Mr. Riley mutters one day to fellow third-grade teacher Mr. Jewel as they stand outside helping with arrivals one morning.

"What? Who are you talking about?" Mr. Jewel replies.

"Students from low-SES families," Mr. Riley says. "Sometimes, they try, but it's just not enough. The communities aren't supportive. We've got to adjust our expectations for these students and realize their success, as far as they can succeed, is on us—us alone. And that's a hard responsibility when the student you are trying to help is throwing chairs and interrupting reading circle!"

Mr. Jewel shakes his head. "It sounds like you've developed a really limiting and very possibly inaccurate mindset. Let me know if you'd like to talk sometime about strategies to support and engage family and community, and about stress relief for yourself!"

Just then, Mr. Riley sees Myra and George arriving to school accompanied by a man with piercings and numerous tattoos showing below his short sleeves. *Who is this?* he wonders. *A transient boyfriend? An unsavory neighbor George and Myra's mother has to rely on because she doesn't have any other options?* "What a day this is going to be," Mr. Riley says to himself.

In this scenario, multiple potential community figures of support exist in George's and Myra's lives. However, Mr. Riley, perhaps through the stress of dealing with George's disruptive behaviors and a lack of clear strategies to address these behaviors, has developed a fixed mindset that no longer allows him to see this potential or imagine ways to engage it. Later, you will see how Mr. Riley's closed mind continues to negatively affect his classroom management and his students' success until he, at last, seeks support to change this mindset and strategies to empower his students through their unique backgrounds rather than dismiss what these backgrounds offer.

Empowering students who live in marginalized communities involves more than guiding them to predetermined ideals about what it means to be successful in school (Seward, 2019). Teachers serve as advocates for their students when they disrupt power imbalances and work to shift power toward people from marginalized communities. Teachers should seek out and develop relationships with individuals in the community who can serve as supports to the students, even if they are not the students' caregivers or immediate family (Milner et al., 2017). Many community members, such as grandparents, godparents, pastors, and—for youth involved in the juvenile justice system—probation officers, are often eager to serve in this role, and students themselves are receptive to the support. The strategies in this book do not present punitive disciplinary measures used to get students to fall in line. Instead, the strategies draw on students' strengths, and the strengths of their families and communities when possible, to support students in fully engaging in the classroom.

While students who live in neighborhoods with limited financial resources can face significant obstacles, it is important to note that students who live in wealthy neighborhoods face their own challenges. These students are more likely to engage in drug and alcohol use and demonstrate internalizing and externalizing problems than students in middle-class neighborhoods are (Luthar, Barkin, & Crossman, 2013). In their journal article "How the Rich Get Riskier," researchers Katelyn F. Romm,

Carolyn McNamara Barry, and Lauren M. Alvis (2020) find that students from affluent families exhibit higher levels of risky behavior than low- and middle-SES youths do. These students engage in risky behavior to navigate the pressures they face while trying to measure up to their parents' exceedingly high expectations for achievement. The study also shows maternal and paternal psychological control has a positive correlation with increased risk-taking behaviors for higher-SES, yet not lower-SES, emerging adults. Research consistently supports that socioeconomic status has a pervasive influence on parents' behavioral and psychological control as well as their helicopter parenting of their children's behaviors. Theories about why this occurs relate to family dynamics, pressure at school, and peer norms. Specifically, the cause may be the immense emphasis that modern culture places on maximizing personal status among youth who live in financially privileged communities. Another theory supports that youth in affluent neighborhoods may engage in more sensation-seeking behavior, such as substance abuse, than youth from middle-class and low-SES neighborhoods do (Jensen, Chassin, & Gonzales, 2017).

Teachers and Schools

School experiences are very influential to students. A cycle of negative interactions can emerge between students with challenging behaviors and their teachers. Specifically, mutual frustration can perpetuate the negative interactions. Additional factors that can impact students' behavior, including authoritarian discipline and zero-tolerance policies, can lead to power struggles with students who already display challenging behaviors. In this chapter's scenario, George struggles with authority figures at school, which often triggers his challenging behaviors.

The range of behaviors school personnel consider acceptable for students is narrow and often unknowingly biased. For example, some educators do not understand how important it might be for students with ADD to take breaks and perhaps stand rather than sit in their designated area in the classroom. If these students are forced to sit at their desks for the majority of their school day, they may unintentionally begin to exhibit disruptive behaviors so they release some built-up energy. Students deserve an honest assessment of how their teachers approach academic instruction, student expectations, and behavior management, and they deserve teachers' willingness to find and communicate flexibility within these approaches when it is possible.

Disproportionality in education, which is defined as the presence of more or fewer students from a specific group in an education program than one would expect based on their representation in the general student population, is a serious issue. It is difficult to determine the specific demographic data of students with challenging behaviors because schools informally identify these students. However, research shows that Black male students are more likely to be referred to the school administration for disciplinary issues than their White counterparts are to be referred to the office for the same incidences (Gregory & Roberts, 2017). There are strategies you can implement to create more successful outcomes for these students. In later chapters, we provide various culturally responsive teaching practices for you to utilize when working with students who have challenging behaviors. Teachers who engage in culturally responsive practices "use what they know, come to understand, and are able to learn in their particular locales with their particular students at particular times" (Milner, Cunningham, Delale-O'Connor, & Kestenberg, 2019, p. 14). That is to say there is no one-size-fits-all approach to working with students who have similar demographics, socioeconomic statuses, or other characteristics. Teachers must develop skills and strategies for interacting with their students based on knowledge about the community in which they teach and the people who live there.

Educators understand that they need to create a nurturing, safe environment to maximize student success within the classroom. But why? The fact is, when students feel respected and valued, they are often more successful academically and exhibit positive behavioral outcomes (Scheuermann & Hall, 2016). At times, teachers may overlook students with challenging behaviors as an asset in the classroom environment, and these students may utilize their teachers as emotional crutches to help navigate their insecurities at school (Hallahan et al., 2019). For example, even though George exhibits challenging behaviors in his classroom and struggles in reading, he is a mathematics wizard. George's classroom teacher, Mr. Riley, often ignores him as a peer mentor in mathematics because of his disruptive behaviors during language arts and reading class periods. In addition, George asks his classroom teacher multiple questions per hour in order to gain the teacher's attention. He also exhibits some learned helplessness during these core subject periods.

Let's see how the pattern George and his teacher have developed perpetuates a negative cycle for both of them.

Mr. Riley reads his third-grade class a story about Oregon Trail pioneers starting out on their big adventure. He asks his students some critical-thinking questions based on the content. George, in a way that Mr. Riley has come to see as typical, begins to interrupt the question-and-answer session with off-topic remarks and attention-seeking questions: "I bet smoked meat tastes icky! How fast can a horse run? I don't like walking!"

Mr. Riley feels increasingly annoyed and angry, but in an attempt to keep the rest of the class on task, he placates George by responding in asides to his remarks and questions. Finally, George makes a comment about the weight that each pioneer wagon pulls and the total weight the group must pull. Mr. Riley recognizes that George is applying ideas he learned in mathematics, and he is impressed; however, by this point, he is too frustrated to engage with George about his observations, so he ignores the comment. George throws his notebook across the room, effectively ending the class discussion for everyone.

As you can see, Mr. Riley misses, or can't develop, a learning opportunity that might engage and empower a student struggling with challenging behaviors, and he doesn't give that student a chance to lead his peers because he directs his energy at mitigating the challenging behaviors themselves. Mr. Riley doesn't have an approach to move beyond damage control, and not having an approach results in frustration for him, his challenging student, and the entire class.

Students with challenging behaviors are included within general education classrooms the majority of the time. However, historically, the education of students with challenging behaviors was viewed as the responsibility of special educators, even if these students were not eligible for special education. In the late 1990s, educators began to see a shift toward proactive systemic approaches that were modeled by response to intervention (RTI; Buffum, Mattos, & Malone, 2018; Fuchs, Fuchs, & Compton, 2010) and positive behavior interventions and supports (PBIS; Horner & Sugai, 2015) frameworks. In the 2020s, educators see these same proactive approaches and consider them to be multitiered systems of support.

Specifically related to shaping student behaviors, PBIS is a framework that emphasizes the use of data-driven, positive, evidence-based practices to decrease challenging behaviors among students and, in effect, increase academic engagement (Center on PBIS, 2022a). In later chapters, we will go into more detail on PBIS and on how the framework can help students who have behavior challenges like George's.

Peers and Peer Groups

Students try to figure out how they are valued within a peer group (Farmer, Reinke, & Brooks, 2014). For example, some peers are valued for being funny, and some are valued for being popular. Some of these students are viewed as funny and popular because of their misconduct while others are seen as rebellious for the same behaviors. These students may rebel against teachers, parents, and other authority figures who attempt to shape their behaviors in order to gain peers' admiration (Farmer et al., 2014).

Students with challenging behaviors can struggle to negotiate friendships with their peers (Farmer et al., 2014). These struggles may involve sportsmanship, personal space, and emotion management. Struggles often take place on school grounds because of continuously evolving social interactions. As such, the challenge of meeting students' social and behavioral needs is a broader responsibility than many individuals realize.

Bullying is a concerning school issue, and the harm bullying can do to students is great. Although bullying occurs within the context of peer interactions, educators should not view bullying as a simple tension among peers. The words *bully* and *peer* are opposites. A peer is considered an equal—a person of the same social standing as oneself—whereas bullying means the bullied student lacks the elements of equality and free choice.

Researchers R. Matthew Gladden, Alana M. Vivolo-Kantor, Merle E. Hamburger, and Corey D. Lumpkin (2014) confirm that the Centers for Disease Control and Prevention released the first federal definition of *bullying*, which has three components: (1) unwanted aggressive behavior, (2) an observed or perceived power imbalance, and (3) repetition of bullying behaviors. Ongoing evaluation of bullying among students in K–12 schools has revealed that all age groups are impacted by bullying; however, bullying seems to be most prominent between the ages of twelve and eighteen. No single profile or demographic of students seems to be bullied over others. Most bullying behaviors occur on school grounds, which makes teachers important in the prevention of bullying among peer groups. Unfortunately, many students with challenging behaviors like those George has also struggle with low academic achievement and are subjects of intense bullying (Gladden et al., 2014).

NATURE

Nurture is quite involved because it encompasses a person's entire environment and how that environment impacts the person's behaviors. While nurture encompasses the environment, *nature* involves genetic or hereditary factors that can impact behavior. In other words, genetics can play a part in one's behavior. Some students are born with or acquire challenging behaviors associated with biological conditions that can contribute to these behaviors (Scott, 2017). Biological factors such as neurological, genetic, and biochemical factors, or a combination of these, can impact behavior. Congenital defects and low birth weight are biological risk factors for children and youth that can contribute to challenging behaviors (Hallahan et al., 2019). Prenatal exposure to environmental toxins, alcohol, or drugs can contribute to various types of disabilities, such as ADD, emotional and behavioral disorders, and learning disabilities.

Neuroimaging techniques such as magnetic resonance imaging (MRI) show researchers that relatively consistent abnormalities appear in several areas of the brain among people with ADD (Hallahan et al., 2019). The frontal lobe, basal ganglia, and cerebellum are the most notable. Researchers have also discovered abnormal levels of dopamine and noradrenaline in individuals with ADD. These chemicals, or neurotransmitters, assist in sending messages between neurons in the brain. There are also structural differences (sizes of various areas of the brain) and functional differences between the brains of people with learning disabilities and those without. While there is not definitive evidence of a neurological basis for all students who are identified as having a learning disability or ADD, evidence points to heredity as playing a strong role in both ADD and learning disabilities, particularly in the case of severe or profound disorders (Hallahan et al., 2019).

Whether neurological difference or heredity factors relate to an individual's diagnosis with ADD or a learning disability, it is rare to find a relationship between one specific biological factor and challenging behaviors. Students with ADD can exhibit challenging behaviors because of the characteristics of ADD, which can include inattention, hyperactivity, and impulsive behaviors. Oftentimes, ADD occurs simultaneously with other behavioral and learning difficulties, including learning disabilities and emotional and behavioral disorders.

Although some challenging behaviors result from biological factors, it is important to find strategies to support the students, and to remember that while everyone is born with a biological predisposition or temperament, there is no direct relationship between temperaments and disorders. As we said earlier, challenging behaviors are any behaviors, or actions, that impede the learning of the students themselves or their peers. Whether students' challenging behavior is a result of nature, nurture, or both, students with challenging behaviors need interventions and strategies to help them be successful academically and socially (Scott, 2017). Teachers can use positive and proactive instruction to effectively set students up for success, rather than waiting for them to fail and then responding to that.

CHALLENGING BEHAVIORS AND ACADEMIC ACHIEVEMENT

Students with challenging behaviors often struggle academically. For example, researchers Victoria L. Joffe and Emma Black (2012) find that students with low academic performance exhibit significantly greater emotional, behavioral, and social difficulties. The relationship between behavior and academic problems has long been recognized; however, although a significant amount of research examines this relationship, there is a lack of evidence to clarify or advance the link between behavior and academic achievement or causes of it (Kremer, Flower, Huang, & Vaughn, 2016).

Seminal work from the distinguished psychologist and author Stephen P. Hinshaw (1992) suggests potential explanations for this relationship. One explanation is that behavior impacts achievement. For example, a student's challenging behavior may prevent the student from fully engaging in the curriculum, causing the student to underperform academically. Another explanation by Hinshaw is that students who struggle academically demonstrate challenging behavior in an attempt to detract from their academic deficiencies. Another explanation is that a third factor could be impacting both behavior and achievement—for example, navigating a pandemic and a change to the home and school environment.

In the past, educators used to focus their attention on behavioral interventions for students with challenging behaviors and exclude academic instruction from these students' school days (Yell et al., 2013). The emphasis for behavior management practices has historically been on the systematic application of consequences after students exhibit challenging behaviors rather than on antecedents (that is, what happens prior to the students' challenging behaviors) or the setting in which the behaviors occur. Research suggests intervention components focusing on academics can positively impact behavior (Wills, Caldarella, Mason, Lappin, & Anderson, 2019). We now understand that quality academic instruction, which is an antecedent, is a highly effective prevention and intervention strategy for students with challenging behaviors. In addition, teachers who are managing students' behaviors can establish a classroom environment that fosters appropriate behaviors (Kauffman & Landrum, 2018). We will further discuss prevention and intervention strategies in this chapter's section titled Preventive Approaches to Challenging Behaviors (page 26).

Teachers must understand that students will often act out or withdraw in frustration at not understanding the curriculum (Yell et al., 2013). Additionally, students may exhibit challenging behaviors if there is a mismatch between instructional delivery styles and students' abilities or needs. You saw this mismatch during Mr. Riley's Oregon Trail reading (page 13). When a mismatch occurs, it may result in a cycle of failure where academic frustrations lead to challenging behaviors, which result in disciplinary practices (for example, time-outs or in-school suspensions) that remove the student from academic instruction. When this happens, the student falls further behind academically and receives fewer opportunities to learn and display appropriate behaviors. This pattern often repeats itself and eventually becomes a chronic situation where the student continues to display challenging behaviors while falling more and more behind academically. For these reasons, it is very important to implement prevention and intervention strategies for antecedents.

OBSTACLES AND APPROACHES TO EFFECTIVELY ADDRESSING CHALLENGING BEHAVIORS

We have talked about students and why they may have challenging behaviors at school. We've also touched on obstacles that can arise when working with students who have challenging behaviors. In this section, we will go into further detail about a few common obstacles that can get in the way of addressing challenging behaviors, *and* we will cover approaches for surmounting these obstacles and effectively addressing the behaviors. When thinking about behavior and specifically challenging behavior, teachers need to dig into not only the cause of the behavior but also the dynamics that surround and support that behavior. For example, they can ask themselves, "Are there things happening in my classroom that may be maintaining the challenging behaviors?" Sometimes, students develop learned helplessness; they feel like if they try, they will just fail again, so what's the point of even trying? Teachers know there is a point to keep trying, but often, their students don't see or feel it. Sometimes, teachers find themselves playing the blame game, where they blame themselves or they blame their students or their students' families or communities, as Mr. Riley began to do in the case of his student, George. Other times, families blame the schools. Ultimately, schools and families need to all work together to do what is best to help students with challenging behaviors be successful in school.

Maintained Consequences

When thinking about challenging behaviors your students exhibit in the classroom, be sure to ask yourself, "Why does the behavior happen? What happens right after the behavior occurs?" And consider whether there are specific consequences or outcomes for maintaining the behavior. Here are some questions to aid you in that consideration (Scott, 2017).

- Do you, as the teacher, provide attention or help in response to the behavior?
- Do you, as the teacher, ignore the behavior?

- Do the student's peers provide attention when the behavior occurs?

- Do the student's peers ignore the behavior?

- Does the student get something enjoyable out of the behavior?

- Does the student use the behavior to avoid work?

- Do the student's peers provide help when the behavior occurs?

Sometimes, the behavior serves more than one purpose. For example, Donna crumples up her mathematics paper and throws it across the room because she doesn't like mathematics. Her teacher sends her to the hall to think about the choice she has made. In the hall, Donna has a perfect view of the cafeteria and what is happening in there. She has avoided doing her work, and she has also gotten something she enjoys, which is watching everyone in the cafeteria.

After Donna's teacher, Ms. Flynn, reads this book, she decides to try a different strategy with Donna. She gives Donna the choice between two mathematics assignments that have the same level of rigor. Ms. Flynn explains to Donna that she gets to decide which assignment she wants to do. Donna starts to argue about it, but Ms. Flynn calmly explains again that she has the choice between the two assignments, tells Donna she will give her a minute to decide, and walks away. A minute later, Ms. Flynn asks Donna what she has decided. Donna picks an assignment and slowly walks back to her seat, where she begins to work. Ms. Flynn walks up to Donna as she is working and tells Donna she is proud of the choice she's made. Donna completes her assignment and is positively reinforced by Ms. Flynn. If Donna had not chosen between the two assignments, Ms. Flynn would have then decided what assignment Donna *would* complete. Ms. Flynn could have also provided other choice options. For example, Ms. Flynn could have given Donna an option of where she could complete the assignment or which type of writing tool she could use to complete the assignment. The idea is to ensure the challenging behavior does not get reinforced by Donna not having to complete the assignment.

Learned Helplessness

Learned helplessness occurs when, after repeated failures, people develop the belief that there is no relationship between their actions in a specific situation and the outcome (Ghasemi, 2021). Consequently, people can believe that negative outcomes are beyond their control (Filippello et al., 2017). As a result, they demonstrate lower motivation to act (Ghasemi, 2021). Students experiencing learned helplessness develop a *fixed mindset* when they exert effort on academic assignments, do not do well on the assignments, and then avoid attempting work in the future to avoid failure. In this scenario, students attribute their failure to a lack of ability (Orkin,

May, & Wolf, 2017). Students avoid work they perceive as challenging because they feel incompetent at successfully completing the work. This can manifest as students' appearing disengaged, unmotivated, or discouraged (Ghasemi, 2021). It often results in failure to complete assigned work or even begin assigned work, or reluctance to participate in whole-class activities and group work. The good news is that you can disrupt the cycle of learned helplessness. The remaining chapters in this book provide practical strategies that you can use to guide students in engaging in academic work via support rather than punishment.

The Blame Game

Causal factors contributing to challenging behaviors can be multidimensional and nuanced. Rather than addressing problematic behaviors with a sense of empathy, knowing they stem from complicated situations, teachers and other school personnel may inadvertently place blame for why the behaviors occur. Consider that from the 1940s to the late 1960s, prominent doctors Leo Kanner (1943) and Bruno Bettelheim (1967) developed and supported the idea of *refrigerator mothers*, placing blame for children's rigid rituals, speech difficulties, and socially withdrawn behaviors squarely on parents' failure to demonstrate parental warmth. Of course, people now know that autism spectrum disorders are complicated neurodevelopmental differences (Al Dera, 2022). Some teachers often still blame disruptive behaviors rooted in attention deficit disorder on "bad" parenting (Gwernan-Jones et al., 2015). As a society, people are often consumed with placing blame for students' problematic behaviors on someone. They typically find themselves condemning the same people: teachers blame themselves, teachers and parents blame students, families blame schools, or schools blame families. The following sections describe these blaming dynamics.

Teachers Blaming Themselves

As a teacher, you are likely your own worst critic. You may wonder on a daily or weekly basis if you can do more to help your students navigate challenging behaviors. Please understand that this self-doubt is typical; however, it is important to find a way to overcome blame and any fear that may arise about not knowing how to help students. You must find a way to accept your students and yourself, and making informed decisions may be the first step to releasing this blame. If you learn a new way to approach challenging behaviors, perhaps you can find your way from blame to proactive problem solving.

Students with challenging behaviors can be intense and require an immense amount of energy, which can create missteps when you are deciding how to proceed. Making mistakes as the manager of your classroom is understandable.

However, do not dwell on mistakes, and move forward with informed decisions and evidence-based practices.

When you blame yourself, as the student's teacher, for your student's challenging behavior, try to remember the following mantra.

> I will accept my students and myself as humans and make informed decisions as the first step to releasing blame. Even if I make a mistake managing my classroom, I will move forward with evidence-based practices.

Teachers and Parents Blaming Students

Teachers and families may be tempted to blame the students for their challenging behaviors and may also be tempted to fault the students for not changing these behaviors themselves. The reality is that students need support to successfully modify problematic behaviors. You may slip into placing blame on your students with challenging behaviors and fail to see the contributing factors, perhaps even how your behavior contributes to the problem.

When you blame a student for his, her, or their challenging behavior, try to remember the following mantra.

> I will accept my students for who they are, but I will understand students are not their challenging behavior. I will see them through this difficult time and move forward with our positive relationship.

Families Blaming Schools

When a student exhibits challenging behaviors, schools and families commonly blame each other. However, educational legislation, such as the Individuals With Disabilities Education Improvement Act (IDEA, 2004) and No Child Left Behind (NCLB, 2001), calls for the cultivation of parent-school cooperative models to promote student success. Before a cooperative model can be created, teachers must first consider cultural differences that may exist between themselves and the students they serve. For example, in some cultures, families hold the belief that school personnel, as trained professionals, should be able to manage their child's behaviors during school hours, especially if the challenging behaviors do not happen at home. If teachers lack understanding of these expectations, they may become defensive and less willing to cooperatively engage with families that hold the school responsible for their child's problematic behaviors. Families and teachers must work together in accordance with best practice and with federal education legislation. In her article titled "Stop the Blame Game," Melissa Davis (2014) outlines five steps to positive parent-teacher collaboration for a student with challenging behaviors.

1. Have parents, teachers, support personnel, and the student come together.

2. Observe the student, and identify a problem behavior. Determine reasons why the problem behavior may occur.

3. Develop a plan to increase positive student behaviors and reduce the problem behavior. Ensure all parties agree to—and implement—the plan.

4. Have parents, teachers, and other personnel communicate regularly on the plan's progress.

5. Determine the success of the plan, and fade out or adjust the interventions as necessary.

When families blame the school for students' challenging behavior, try to remember the following mantra.

> Schools need help from the families to better understand the students with challenging behaviors in order to foster positive relationships.

Schools Blaming Families

Ruth Colker (2015) serves as an advocate for legal guardians who have children and youth receiving special education services in public school systems. She recounts numerous phone calls and interviews with family members, mainly mothers, who feel schools consistently blame them for their children's misconduct. In addition, the schools claim these parents lie to their children's teachers.

After Colker (2015) found this significant trend between schools and families, she decided to investigate and report the schools' treatment of families, specifically mothers. Interestingly, Colker (2015) found a few trends. We have added examples of ways these trends may manifest themselves to the following list.

• A school district disrespects a family member's disability. For example, school personnel neglect to offer multiple communication options to a deaf parent.

- A school district blames a family member's assertive behavior for the student's academic and behavioral issues at school. For example, the school district neglects to identify a student who demonstrates significant challenging behavior as having a disability; instead, the district blames the mother for supporting her child's intentional problematic behavior.

- A school district blames a family member for being too passive. For example, school administration blames a mother who has difficulty reading and understanding all her child's individualized education program (IEP) documents for her son's lack of educational progress. However, it is found that the school has not been providing services mandated in the IEP.

- A school district places unrealistic expectations on working parents or guardians. For example, the school district denies a mother's request for her child, who demonstrates significantly challenging behavior, to receive a nonpublic, segregated placement because the mother took a three-week leave of absence to stay home with her child full-time, and the child did exceptionally well during that time.

Colker's (2015) investigations make it clear that schools may seem disgruntled with parents or guardians if they appear to be too pushy, too passive, or too helpful. Again, the educational legislation is devised to create a cooperative model between families and schools. Both families and schools must remember to treat each other with dignity and respect to provide the most successful outcomes for students with challenging behaviors.

Moving forward, we want schools to stop playing the blame game. We want them to consider that families, teachers, and students all benefit from empathy and support. Also consider that placing blame for a student's challenging behaviors may prolong your inability to move forward and effectively implement evidence-based practices that will positively impact the student's behaviors within the home and school environments.

When you blame your student's family for the challenging behavior, try to remember the following mantra.

> Raising a child is not easy, and families are likely doing the best they can. I will accept my student and the student's family for who they are and move forward with our positive relationships.

Blaming various people in students' lives is an obstacle to effectively addressing challenging and disruptive behaviors and, ultimately, to helping the students become happier, better adjusted, and academically competent.

Matters of Mindset

It's important to understand why students have challenging behaviors and to remember that different students will have challenging behaviors for different reasons. Once you have a good understanding of why students may exhibit challenging behaviors, you can figure out how you, as a classroom teacher, can help. If students continue to display problem behaviors, despite your putting supports in place, you have to consider whether specific consequences or outcomes are maintaining the difficult behaviors. You can help once you figure this out.

Additionally, you must remember to think about your own mindset and the impact an educator mindset can have. Working with students who have challenging behaviors is not easy. Teachers report high rates of stress, burnout, and emotional burden and find student misbehavior to be a common source of stress (Wink, LaRusso, & Smith, 2021). Days when teachers' patience is limited can lead to overwhelm, and then to damaging mindsets that may involve blame, pessimism, and rigid thinking. A great way to begin to combat these damaging mindsets is to exercise simple self-awareness, staying cognizant of the need to be self-aware and check in mentally with the ways you are feeling, thinking, and responding. This awareness can allow you to experience the internal locus of control that you need to adjust your mindset and your actions.

When teachers have a growth mindset, they believe their students' personal characteristics (such as their intellectual abilities and their behavior) can be developed (Yeager & Dweck, 2020). When you, as a teacher, have a growth mindset, you can influence your students' motivation and achievement. A growth mindset can also help you be more empathetic toward your students with challenging behaviors. Being able to empathize with students' perspectives and life experiences better equips you to handle problem behaviors, use effective problem-solving strategies, and lower any job burnout (Wink et al., 2021).

After you develop self-awareness, the big question becomes, How do you build on it to foster a growth mindset in yourself so you can best support your students with challenging behaviors? Justin D. Garwood, Christopher L. Van Loan, and Margaret Gessler Werts (2017) wrote an article on the mindset of paraprofessionals serving students with challenging behaviors. In their article, they delineate twelve survival mindsets from the seminal work of Jo Webber, Tom Anderson, and Laura Otey (1991), who wrote about the importance of a teacher's mindset (self-efficacy, hope) when working with students who have challenging behaviors. Following are the twelve mindsets detailed by Garwood and colleagues (2017).

1. When there is a problem, always believe there is an answer (Webber et al., 1991). In other words, you can't give up on students with challenging behaviors. You need to seek out help and ask questions.

2. Try to find the positives in negative circumstances (Webber et al., 1991). Although you need to acknowledge negative situations when they occur, you can't focus on them. It is important to remain optimistic.

3. Be mindful to learn what function a student's behavior serves for the student (Webber et al., 1991). To best help meet the student's needs, you need to try to see things from the student's perspective.

4. Celebrate even the little things (Webber et al., 1991). Remind yourself and believe that any amount of progress is still progress, no matter how small it is.

5. Believe that conflicts can foster opportunities for growth (Webber et al., 1991). You need to understand that conflicts with a student may sometimes occur because you are getting to the root cause of the problem behaviors.

6. Although it can be challenging, don't take your students' behaviors personally (Webber et al., 1991). When students blow up at you or act like they don't care, don't assume they don't like you.

7. To best help your students, explore all potential avenues (Webber et al., 1991). Step outside your comfort zone and try new things to help your students.

8. Remember that mistakes will happen (Webber et al., 1991). Teachers make mistakes, and so do students. Accept the fact that things won't always go the way you originally planned.

9. Downtime is not good (Webber et al., 1991). A great way to be proactive and prevent problem behaviors from occurring is to plan engaging academic activities.

10. Overcome the fear of physical or emotional pain brought on by students (Webber et al., 1991). You must stop and ask for help. This is particularly true if you find yourself driven by fear of personal pain or failure.

11. Embrace the strange and funny side of life (Webber et al., 1991). Having a good sense of humor can help you neutralize negative circumstances and connect with students.

12. There are times when you need to challenge and change your irrational thoughts (Webber et al., 1991). It can be challenging, but it's important to not let yourself become obsessed with negativity and doomsday scenarios.

A growth mindset can foster resilience in yourself, giving you the necessary mental foundation to help your students develop resilience as well, and from resilience, academic engagement and success.

PREVENTIVE APPROACHES TO CHALLENGING BEHAVIORS

The following two preventive and proactive approaches to supporting students— (1) the positive behavior interventions and supports (PBIS) framework and (2) cultural responsiveness—are particularly important. These approaches help set the foundation for the evidence-based practices in this book, as each practice is rooted in PBIS and in cultural responsiveness.

Positive Behavior Interventions and Supports

Many educators are familiar with the term response to intervention, or RTI, which is a multitiered framework that addresses academic functioning in students. Each tier provides additional supports (Buffum et al., 2018; RTI Action Network, n.d.). While RTI is a multitiered framework to support students academically, PBIS is a multitiered framework to support students with their behaviors. PBIS is a response to the growing need for a more proactive approach to school discipline (Scheuermann & Hall, 2016). To address this need, PBIS, much like RTI, helps educational professionals take a prevention-versus-intervention approach in working with all students. Educators understand preventing challenging behaviors is most important; however, educators sometimes inevitably have to intervene to modify these behaviors. Robert H. Horner and George Sugai (2015) describe PBIS as a proactive and preventive implementation framework to increase all students' academic and behavioral outcomes in educational settings. This framework emphasizes the importance of using data to make informed decisions about programming, applying evidence-based practices, and having systems that increase positive behavior change among all students (Center on PBIS, 2022a).

PBIS makes a positive impact at the school, classroom, and individual levels because school personnel are being proactive and preventive rather than reactive

(Center on PBIS, 2022a). The impact is made possible because all stakeholders understand and implement PBIS in educational environments. These stakeholders, who have a vested interest in the ultimate success of the school's students, may include the following.

- School administrators
- Classroom teachers
- Parents or guardians
- Students
- Paraprofessionals
- Mental health clinicians
- Custodians
- Cafeteria workers
- Bus drivers

The PBIS framework encompasses three tiers (Center on PBIS, 2022a). Tier 1 involves proactively meeting the needs of all students. At this level, students learn classroom rules and procedures, which teachers reinforce with incentives such as tokens or specific praise and consequences that are natural and match the behaviors. Expectations are clear and consistent (Center on PBIS, 2022b). Despite having a wonderful, positive, and proactive plan, some students will at times still struggle with their behavior. These students move to tier 2, where they receive support at tier 1 and support at tier 2. Students move to tier 2 because they need more than tier 1 support and are at risk for developing more serious challenging behaviors (Center on PBIS, 2022c). Students at tier 2 need more targeted interventions, such as increased adult supervision, increased access to academic support, and an increased focus on understanding the function of the students' challenging behaviors. If a student continues to struggle despite all mechanisms in place, the student moves to tier 3 for individualized and intensive support (Center on PBIS, 2022d). Teachers may conduct a functional behavioral assessment to determine why the student is acting in the disruptive way. Then teachers do person-centered planning to determine how to best help individual students. It is important, in this planning, to consider the student's and school's culture and context (that is, neighborhoods and personal characteristics).

Figure 1.1 (page 28) depicts the three tiers, the continuum of support, and the tiers' function with all students. Note that implementing PBIS within a classroom or school comes with various barriers. These barriers can include teacher resistance to implementation, lack of resources, insufficient buy-in among all stakeholders within the framework, logistic barriers like inadequate data collection, and inconsistent implementation, to name a few.

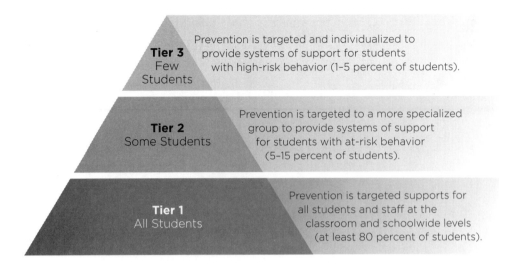

Tier 3
Few Students
Prevention is targeted and individualized to provide systems of support for students with high-risk behavior (1–5 percent of students).

Tier 2
Some Students
Prevention is targeted to a more specialized group to provide systems of support for students with at-risk behavior (5–15 percent of students).

Tier 1
All Students
Prevention is targeted supports for all students and staff at the classroom and schoolwide levels (at least 80 percent of students).

Figure 1.1: Continuum of schoolwide instructional and positive behavior interventions and supports.

Here's an example of PBIS in use: Ms. Bullock is setting up her fourth-grade general education classroom at Nichols Elementary School with the principles of the PBIS framework. She first creates a checklist to develop the tier 1 foundation of the PBIS framework within her classroom plan. Her checklist includes the following three steps.

1. Organize the physical space.

2. Manage behavior.

    a. Establishing rules and procedures

    b. Establishing a reinforcement system

    c. Establishing accountability among students

3. Create academic instruction.

For step 1, Ms. Bullock understands that the physical environment of her classroom needs to be a positive learning refuge for her students. She organizes her students' desks and chairs based on her philosophy of teaching (for example, small-group instruction and reading centers). She constructs her daily routines and activity stations to create a seamless flow within her classroom. For example, Ms. Bullock has a pencil-sharpening area in the classroom with all necessary items. She has file folders labeled for each subject area and time of the day. She has an area for her bathroom passes and student checkout forms. Finally, she has a seating chart for her class and is prepared to revise it as she becomes more familiar with her students and their needs. For example, as she gets to know her students, she will learn which students can work best together and which students need to move spots.

For step 2, after Ms. Bullock creates an inviting classroom environment for her students, she collaboratively establishes the classroom rules and posts them. As advised by Harry and Rosemary Wong's (2018) famous work for new and novice teachers, *The First Days of School*, Ms. Bullock works with her students to create three to five classroom rules. Ms. Bullock understands that when her students have the opportunity to create their classroom rules, they feel a sense of ownership and pride. She also discusses and explicitly teaches, models, and reinforces the daily procedures (for example, sharpening pencils, taking bathroom breaks, and submitting classwork) for her students throughout the school year. She wants to develop a consistent pattern with her students to reduce problematic behaviors.

With fully developed classroom rules and procedures, Ms. Bullock understands it is time to establish how she will reinforce her students. She decides to follow her schoolwide PBIS framework and provide her students with the school's tangible reinforcement of Nichols nickels (which chapter 3, page 55, will further describe). The goal of reinforcement is for the student to work for an intrinsic reinforcement of completing a task (Scheuermann & Hall, 2016); however, this extrinsic reinforcement is a good start. Based on this schoolwide system, students earn Nichols nickels from stakeholders in the building for various positive behaviors. For example, Ms. Bullock may distribute a Nichols nickel to one of her students, DeMarcus, for appropriately asking for help. Ms. Holt, the assistant principal, may give DeMarcus a Nichols nickel for staying in his assigned area during his lunch break. At the end of the week, DeMarcus will be able to spend his Nichols nickels on various desired reinforcements at the school store, such as a vending-machine pass or a no-shoes pass. Ms. Bullock will also continue with verbal praise to reinforce positive behaviors. This decision is not only supported by evidence from her own experience but also backed by research. The Center on PBIS (2022a) recommends that classroom teachers acknowledge positive student behaviors at least five times more often than they acknowledge problematic student issues. Research has long supported that students, particularly students with challenging behaviors, react more productively to reinforcement than to punitive measures such as detention, no recess, or reduced points (Lewis & Sugai, 1999; Zaheer et al., 2019).

Ms. Bullock also understands that holding her students accountable for their behaviors is an important step in her classroom. She plans to continue her positive reinforcement with her students and implement consequences for classroom rule infractions. Ms. Bullock understands that consistency is key. Her students should be able to predict what will happen if they do not meet a classroom rule or expectation (Scott, 2017). Ms. Bullock plans to make sure her consequences are brief, delivered with a compassionate demeanor, and specific to the problem behavior. She also wants to make sure consequences are consistent for all her students.

Finally, Ms. Bullock wants to create stimulating classroom instruction for her students. This positive student engagement will minimize problematic behaviors (Scott, 2017). In fact, once she establishes her behavioral management plan, Ms. Bullock will be able to focus on high-quality instruction. She can ensure that her instruction is rigorous and differentiated to meet the diverse needs of her students.

In the PBIS framework, Ms. Bullock's plan fits within tier 1 because she has created a positive, proactive plan for all her students. Her plan will prevent most challenging behaviors from occurring in her classroom. However, some of her students will have more extensive needs, and Ms. Bullock will support them as she draws from strategies aligned with tier 2 and tier 3 in the PBIS framework.

Cultural Responsiveness

In this book, we define *culture* as the way of life of groups of people, describing how they do things. Students and their families, peers, and schools are embedded in cultures that influence them (Hallahan et al., 2019). Specifically, people are all influenced by their own cultural perspectives, which impact how they react to various situations. Adults' cultural viewpoints affect how they interact with children and youth as well as what expectations they have for them. The same can be said about students' interactions with and expectations of not only the adults in their lives but also their peers. Students are more culturally influenced by their families and schools at a young age, but as they get older, cultural influence shifts to the community and peers. Also, related to this chapter's Nurture section (page 6), understanding the ways different cultures hold different views about children and education builds empathy for differences that can be supportive for students.

Cultural responsivity is a crucial element of this book, and therefore, each strategy is accompanied by information and examples about how to implement the strategy in a culturally responsive way. Becoming a culturally responsive teacher takes intentionality, and it looks different from classroom to classroom and from teacher to teacher.

Let's revisit the Myra and George scenario one last time to see how Mr. Riley finally moves forward in effectively addressing George's challenging behaviors.

> Mr. Riley feels like he's reaching a breaking point. Every interaction he has with George is fraught with tension and disruption. He feels like he's in a nerve-racking power struggle with George. As the adult and teacher, he knows he's responsible for breaking the pattern of behavior, but he is not sure how to do that. If he's entirely honest with himself, he's able to release

some of his tension by blaming the chaos of George's family, and blaming others has started to feel good. That scares him. "Here comes the questionable neighbor doing drop-off duty again," he laments to Mr. Jewel as they once again stand outside the school, greeting the students as they arrive.

Mr. Jewel squints toward George and Myra. "Your student looks happy with that guy," he says. "Have you thought about asking George about his relationship with the family friend? Or asking him about what he likes to do outside of school?"

Mr. Riley grumbles in reply, but almost before he knows what he's doing, he walks over to George, Myra, and their family friend who is dropping them off. He puts out a hand. "Hi," Mr. Riley says. "I'm Mr. Riley, George's third-grade teacher. It's a pleasure to meet you and good to see George looking so happy."

Several days later, Mr. Riley thinks back on all the things that changed for the better in a short period of time because he took initiative to adjust his own behavior and mindset. He learned that the family friend, named Joe, is an important mentor to George. Joe owns a small bicycle-repair shop near where George's family lives. He runs a program through which he restores bicycles and gifts them to formerly incarcerated young men so that they have a way to travel to new jobs. Joe sometimes allows George to help him work on repairing the bicycles. With his mechanical and mathematical bent, this is a real treat for George. "I know how to use an Allen wrench!" George shouted, jumping up and down.

"The bicycle program literally offers a vehicle to success," Joe said.

Mr. Riley can't stop thinking about these words: "vehicle to success." Later, he talks to his principal about what he's learned about George, and together, they design an introduce-your-mentor day for all the third-grade students. Of course, George chooses to introduce Joe.

Several months later, the school has also implemented a family potluck day. George and Myra both revel in the chance to show off their beloved grandmother and everything she has taught them about cooking. At the end of the potluck, George's grandmother takes out a box of discount doughnuts and hands it to George. "If there are eight doughnuts in the box and twenty-four people in your class, how do you need to divide the doughnuts so that everyone gets the same amount?" she asks him.

"In thirds!" George shrieks with excitement before suddenly turning serious. "Well, actually, I'd need to divide them in a little bit less than thirds because there are *twenty-five* people who would need doughnuts." And as he says this, he points at his teacher, Mr. Riley. Tears come to Mr. Riley's eyes. Everyone enjoys the doughnuts that day!

Mr. Riley's efforts at addressing George's disruptive behaviors are ultimately successful because he finds a way to recognize and appreciate George's cultural and family background and to engage George's unique interests and talents in the learning experience. Additionally, Mr. Riley, in creating scenarios that help George succeed, ends up developing programs that offer tier 1 support to all students in the school.

It is our hope that over time, and with repeated practice, you will become proficient in supporting your students in ways that are meaningful and meet their diverse and unique needs. It is equally important to draw on the assets each student brings to the classroom and to build on those assets when developing ways to provide support.

CONCLUDING THOUGHTS

There is always a reason why challenging behavior occurs. When teachers learn why behaviors can occur, it helps them in their work with students who exhibit challenging behaviors. Remember, it is not possible to determine one specific factor causing problem behaviors. Numerous factors working together can result in challenging behaviors (Hallahan et al., 2019). It is essential to keep in mind that different factors will probably contribute to the challenging behaviors of the students in your classroom, and a strategy that helps one student may not be helpful for another.

The seven evidence-based practices that follow can help educators navigate the complexity of their students' problematic classroom behaviors related to academic engagement. We understand all students' environments, strengths, and needs are varied. In addition, teachers manage their classrooms differently. However, the seven evidence-based strategies will hopefully maximize appropriate behaviors and increase academic success. Some strategies we discuss are more prevention based (tier 1) while others are intervention based (tier 2). Some of the evidence-based practices can be both prevention and intervention based. In each case, we walk you through things to consider as you think about implementation, such as being culturally responsive and thinking about students' interests. As you read, there may be strategies you love and others you do not, and that's OK! We want you to find the strategies that work for you because, ultimately, they will help your students be successful.

Chapter 1: Questions for Reflection

Write your responses to the following questions. Keep these responses in mind as you work to address challenging student behaviors and guide your students toward academic engagement and motivated learning.

1. At the beginning of this chapter, we asked you what problematic student behaviors occur in your classroom. Now that you have read chapter 1, what factors do you think may be contributing to these problematic behaviors in your students?

2. Why is it important that educators create a nurturing, safe environment for students?

3. Students with challenging behaviors may struggle interpersonally among their peers and educators in school. How can you help mitigate these issues within your classroom?

4. Research finds that academic deficiencies and student behavioral struggles are often related. How can educators help address this pattern among students with challenging behaviors?

5. Reflect on your students' challenging behaviors in your classroom. What would you theorize is sustaining these behaviors?

6. How can you help prevent learned helplessness among your students?

7. What steps can educators take to prevent themselves from blaming others for students' challenging behaviors?

8. What are positive behavior interventions and supports that you have implemented or could implement within your classroom?

9. Why is it important for all stakeholders to be involved with the PBIS framework?

10. How can an understanding of students' cultural backgrounds influence your teaching, particularly of students with challenging behaviors?

Chapter 2

Students Would Like a Choice: A Guide to Providing Choices

Charlie is a carefree, fun-loving eleventh-grade student who attends an urban high school. He lives with his grandmother DeeDee and his beloved dog, Gigi. He takes three city buses to and from school each day. He works at a local fast-food restaurant from 4:30 p.m. to 10:00 p.m. most weekday nights.

Charlie enjoys socializing with his friends, spending time with his dog, and gaming, and his favorite subject in school is language arts. His teachers enjoy his sense of humor and his love of life. However, he can be quite difficult at times due to his challenging behaviors in the classroom, specifically when he is asked to complete his independent work in mathematics, science, and social studies classes. He often yells, sulks, or refuses to complete his classwork during this independent work time, and his teachers in these three classes are frustrated.

The three teachers finally decide to meet to discuss strategies they could implement with Charlie in their classrooms to help minimize these problematic behaviors. Charlie's teachers decide on the strategy of providing choices as an intervention that will help Charlie when he is confronted with his independent work; however, each teacher chooses to provide choices differently. Since Charlie is a secondary student and can effectively engage and participate in conversations regarding his education, the three teachers inform Charlie they will begin implementing these choices with him in their classrooms to help reduce his challenging behaviors. He asks what this means, and the teachers give examples of the different kinds of choices they will offer. In addition, they all agree to collect data on the strategy of implementing choices with Charlie for six weeks. At the end of the six weeks, they will reconvene to discuss Charlie's behavioral and academic progress in their classrooms.

Being offered choices helps students develop a sense of control and self-determination, which, in turn, prevents problem behaviors from occurring. When students are told what to do all day long, it can make them feel angry or frustrated or even trapped in a cycle of negativity that they think will lead to a bad outcome they feel powerless to prevent. These feelings can result in students' acting out in the classroom. When students receive choices throughout their school day and feel more empowered in their learning, they can feel a greater sense of control over their lives. The sense of control and self-determination derived from having a choice can be particularly important for students with disabilities, whose unique challenges often lead to more limited opportunities to make choices than their same-age peers receive (Skerbetz & Kostewicz, 2013). Research shows that when students—all students—receive opportunities for choice, they have feelings of autonomy and motivation as well as increased engagement and academic achievement (Patall, Cooper, & Wynn, 2010). Research also indicates that having a choice supports decreased problem behaviors and increased task engagement (Jolivette, Ennis, & Swoszowski, 2017).

This chapter, built on a foundation of this research, shows how educators can give students choices by articulating the data-collecting process that informs the context in which choice is best offered. It also shows how educators can respect students' experiences by considering cultural and linguistic diversity, how they can make students active participants in choice selection, and ways they can reinforce the impact of choice. The chapter wraps up with a Concluding Thoughts section and a reproducible page that includes reflective questions to ponder. The chapter will revisit the Charlie scenario throughout to make the concepts of the chapter visible within an imaginary school context.

HOW TO IMPLEMENT CHOICE

So how do you start the practice of offering your students choices within the often-prescribed parameters of a class, school day, or unit of study? You start by employing the sort of thinking and acting discussed in the introduction (page 1) and chapter 1 (page 5) of this book. That means using observation to collect data on where and how problem behaviors usually occur, which students need choices most, and what elements of a school day you can glean for appropriate choices, for example. Collecting data is the first action in the following choice implementation process. Data collection allows you to better understand what choice options would be most appropriate for the student. When thinking about choice options, you also need to consider cultural and linguistic diversity. Involving the student in the process will help ensure you meet the student's needs. Being involved in reinforcement ideas makes the ideas more meaningful to the student.

Following are the four steps you will take to implement choice.

1. **Collect data:** Use observation and applicable tools to gather data prior to implementing choice with your students. You will focus on what problem behaviors you are seeing in your class and in what contexts they occur, which students need choice (or which need it most), and which elements of class time or the learning process can be accessed in various ways and thus offer choices to students.

2. **Consider cultural and linguistic diversity:** Develop relationships with students that open communication and promote understanding of and respect for their cultural experiences and personal preferences. This way, you can further strengthen the impact of offering choice.

3. **Involve students in choice selection:** Guide students to become active participants in choice selection by discussing their challenges and preferences.

4. **Review ideas for reinforcement:** Articulate and examine ways to maintain the positive outcomes of student choice by offering appropriate reinforcements to the choice process. You may do so by once again involving students in a selection process and redeploying data collection techniques.

Collect Data

Before implementing choices for students or groups of students with challenging behaviors, you must identify the problem activities, or the context or setting for the problem behaviors. For example, how often does the challenging behavior cause disruptions or lead to office referrals? Or, how often and when is the student engaged in appropriate behaviors? By collecting data, you learn where and when the noncompliance or task refusal occurs most and least often (Landrum & Sweigart, 2014). Two handy ways a teacher can collect data are by (1) completing an event recording or (2) completing a scatterplot. Both options are quick and easy to implement.

An event recording involves noting each time the behavior occurs. Event recording allows you to easily collect data for a short amount of time. A downside of using event recording is that if you do not do multiple event recordings, you will find it hard to get a clear picture of when, where, and why challenging behaviors are occurring. A scatterplot is based on the student's entire week and involves making marks when the behaviors of concern occur within that specific time period. A scatterplot provides a clearer picture because you do it over a week's time. However, this is more time intensive because you collect data throughout the entire day and week.

Following are examples of a completed event recording sheet and a completed scatterplot (figure 2.1 and figure 2.2). If a student has one teacher for most of the day, that teacher can collect data. However, if the student has more than one teacher, the teachers need to communicate to determine whether the challenging behaviors are happening in all classes or just some classes. Data should be collected in all classes to gain a clear understanding of when and where the behaviors are occurring.

Event Recording

Student's name: Milo   **Date:** 5/16

Observer: Mrs. Sass

Observable behavior: Milo gets out of his seat during independent work time.

Time interval: 10:30 to 10:50   **Total time:** 20 minutes

Frequency (circle one number for each observation):

① ② ③ ④ ⑤ ⑥ ⑦ ⑧ ⑨ ⑩ ⑪ ⑫ ⑬ ⑭ ⑮ ⑯ ⑰ ⑱ ⑲ ⑳

㉑ 22 23 24 25 26 27 28 29 30 31 32 33 34 35

Notes: When Milo got up, he talked to other students at their tables, sharpened his pencil, went to get papers off the counter, or asked the teacher a question.

Figure 2.1: Event recording example.

*Visit **go.SolutionTree.com/behavior** for a free reproducible version of this figure.*

Scatterplot Assessment

Student: Audra   **Observer:** Mr. Kisamore   **Date:** 3/28

Target behavior: Refusal to comply with teacher directions by crumpling paper, putting head on desk, or saying no in a raised voice

Mark **/** if the target behavior was observed one time.

Mark **X** if the target behavior was observed two to three times.

Mark ■ if the target behavior was observed four or more times.

Mark nothing if the target behavior was not observed.

Mark **n/a** if the target behavior is nonapplicable (for whatever reason).

TIME	Monday	Tuesday	Wednesday	Thursday	Friday
8:00–8:30 a.m.	/	■	■	■	/
8:30–9:00 a.m.	X	/	/	/	/
9:00–9:30 a.m.	X	/	/	/	/
9:30–10:00 a.m.	■	■	X	X	/
10:00–10:30 a.m.					
10:30–11:00 a.m.					
11:00–11:30 a.m.	/	X	X	■	■
11:30 a.m.–12:00 p.m.		X			
12:00–12:30 p.m.		X	/	/	
12:30–1:00 p.m.			/		
1:00–1:30 p.m.	X		/	X	/
1:30–2:00 p.m.	■				
2:30–3:00 p.m.	X	■	■	X	

Figure 2.2: Scatterplot assessment example.

Visit **go.SolutionTree.com/behavior** *for a free reproducible version of this figure.*

Once you have ascertained the frequency and location of a student's challenging behaviors, you will need to determine what is happening when the student displays the challenging behaviors. Let's revisit the chapter-opening scenario to see what the data collected by Charlie's mathematics teacher, Ms. Foster, tell her about which situations challenge Charlie and how implementing choice can help Charlie gain a measure of control in these situations.

> Ms. Foster, the teacher with whom Charlie seems to have the most strife, collects data using a scatterplot data collection sheet. She determines that Charlie's challenging behaviors tend to occur when students are independently working on mathematics problems at the end of class. She typically gives Charlie and his peers twenty problems to complete at the end of each mathematics class. During this time, Ms. Foster circulates around the classroom and offers help to those students who need additional support. Charlie's challenging behaviors often involve refusal to begin or to complete the work, noncompliance when prompted to work, and use of profanity.
>
> Mr. Woodruff, Charlie's science teacher, also observes Charlie's challenging behaviors within his classroom during independent work times.
>
> In addition, Ms. Hurst, Charlie's social studies teacher, observes instances of Charlie's challenging behaviors (for example, refusal to work, disgruntlement when prompted to work, and profanity directed at adults) during independent work time. However, she observes fewer challenging behaviors than her colleagues do. She surmises this is because social studies is more closely aligned with language arts (Charlie's favorite subject) than mathematics and science are.

At some point in their career, all teachers have worked or will work with a student like Charlie. Providing choices for students like Charlie allows them to feel a sense of freedom and power with their education. In addition, it allows these students the autonomy to decide the route in which they will learn new skills. As you read, Charlie struggles with his independent work times, specifically in mathematics. When his teacher implements choice for Charlie, he can feel more empowered by choosing how he completes this work.

Teachers may utilize the evidence-based practice of implementing choice with students who fall within PBIS framework tiers 1 and 2. Choice may also be appropriate for students who move to tier 3. Research states students best benefit from choices in their daily classwork (Scheuermann & Hall, 2016). When coupled with reinforcement, choosing their preferences in the classroom gives joy to students like Charlie.

After you collect data on when and where a student's challenging behaviors occur, it is time to set the parameters for the choices you might allow the student. Creating a selection of choices likely starts with considering the contexts in which the challenging behaviors take place. Charlie, for example, typically acts in a disruptive way during independent work time. This could indicate that he feels a need for greater guidance, is struggling with the material, or learns best in a more interactive situation, for instance. A teacher of a student like Charlie then may draft choice selections that include, for example, working with a teacher by one's side for part of independent work time, choosing a format by which to review lesson concepts (such as play a mathematics game based on the concepts, watch a YouTube video about the concepts, or refer to textbook material), and working with a peer for part of independent work time. The teacher may modify these choice options after a discussion with the student.

In addition to considering the viability of possible choices, teachers should consider the classroom environment, rules, policies, goals, classroom climate, peer groups, and so on before offering choices. Teachers would best provide choices within these factors' parameters to their students who have challenging behaviors.

Consider Cultural and Linguistic Diversity

Implementing choice is naturally culturally responsive because students receive the opportunity to choose the materials, reinforcers, and so on that they most identify with (Edwards, 2011). Culturally responsive teaching requires getting to know students academically and personally to develop significant relationships with them and their families (Edwards & Edick, 2013). Developing relationships (such as by using the strategies in table 2.1, page 42) allows for open communication. It promotes student and family involvement in designing appropriate educational experiences and understanding student interests when creating choice options. Providing options based on students' interests, strengths, and cultures is more meaningful than offering choices that the teacher develops in isolation. Additionally, for students whose native language is not English, the teacher may need to present choice options in a language other than English.

The how-to strategies in table 2.1 are useful to apply throughout work with students, and teachers can revisit them as important reminders when reviewing data on challenging student behaviors, considering choice options, and entering into a discussion about choice selection with students.

Table 2.1: Strategies for Developing Significant Relationships With Students and Families

Idea	How-To
Know Your Students as Individuals	• Learn your students' names, and make certain that you are pronouncing the names correctly. • Learn at least three tidbits of information about each student (favorite video game, best friend, favorite sports team, or favorite musician, band, or group). • Refrain from expressing negative judgment if you are not a fan of a favorite of theirs.
Involve Families	• Seek family input about class reading material. • Develop specific opportunities for families to be involved in their children's schoolwork, assignments, and projects. • Distribute a survey to find out what families expect of you. • Send out a class newsletter in the languages spoken by your students' families.
Learn About Different Interaction Styles	• Consider variations in how people of different cultures interact. For example, in some cultures, avoiding eye contact and expressing disagreement with someone while that person is still talking are behavioral expectations, not disrespectful student behaviors. • Know that English learners may be very reluctant to answer questions during a class discussion even if they appear to have strong verbal skills during social interactions.
Develop a Community of Trust in Your Classroom	• Before students are to answer a question aloud, let them work on the answer with a peer. • When a student gives an incorrect answer, praise the effort and avoid criticizing the student. • For students who are very reluctant to answer questions aloud in class, set them up for success by calling on them only when you are certain they know the correct answer.

Involve Students in Choice Selection

Once the teacher has collected data and considered choice possibilities and cultural and linguistic diversity, the teacher needs to involve the student in making choice selections. The teacher must privately discuss with the student the idea of implementing choice. For example, teachers may ask students to eat lunch with them or meet up with them at another free time in the day. During that time, the teacher can explain choice and how it will be implemented in the classroom. The teacher should encourage the student to ask questions and provide ideas for reinforcements they would like to earn. Once the teacher has ascertained what choices are available to the student, the teacher and student can develop a list of reasonable choices the student might select. In their meeting, the student and teacher will agree on the list of choices and reinforcements, and then the teacher will provide the choice options throughout the day. Table 2.2 shares various examples of choices teachers and students could develop in elementary and secondary settings.

Table 2.2: Examples of Teacher- and Student-Developed Choices

Student's Challenging Behavior	Context or Setting	Teacher- and Student-Developed Choices
Emilio, Second Grade		
When Emilio is provided independent science classwork, he often refuses to complete the assignment.	Emilio discusses with his teacher that he finds science challenging, and he would prefer to get the teacher's help during his independent classwork time.	Emilio and his teacher discuss his choices for when he is assigned independent science classwork. Emilio will be able to choose to sit with his teacher during half of his independent science classwork time and ask questions. He will have to complete the other half of the assignment on his own.
Ava, Fourth Grade		
When Ava transitions from one classroom to another, she yells in the hallways and is tardy to class.	Ava explains to her homeroom teacher that the large groups of students transitioning to their classes make her anxious.	Ava and her homeroom teacher discuss her choices for transitioning to other classes. Ava will be able to choose to leave class one minute before the bell sounds or to put her headphones on during the transition.
Dylan, Ninth Grade		
When Dylan is provided a writing assignment, he distracts his peers and avoids his assignment.	Dylan expresses to his teacher that he requires a quiet place when he has to complete a writing assignment.	Dylan and his teacher discuss his choices for writing assignments. He will be able to choose the area in the classroom where he will complete his writing assignments.

continued →

Valentina, Twelfth Grade		
When Valentina is asked to stay in her designated area during mathematics class, she continues to roam the classroom.	Valentina reveals to her mathematics teacher that she roams the classroom to spend more time with her best friend. She can see her best friend only during mathematics class and would like to spend more time with her, if possible.	Valentina and her teacher discuss her choices for during mathematics class. She will be able to choose to sit and work with her best friend only during small-group instruction.

Choice is implemented in one context or setting at a time, with the teacher giving the student one choice from the established list prior to each problem activity or scenario. It is important to vary the offered choices to prevent boredom. If data show providing choices is effective, then teachers can offer choice in various contexts as appropriate. They will know choice is effective when problem behaviors decrease, appropriate behaviors increase, and the student completes the desired academic tasks. If data show a high rate of challenging behaviors remains, then teachers need to determine why that is and what needs to change to increase appropriate behaviors.

Let's go back to the Charlie example. Charlie and his teachers work together to come up with the best choice options for their individual classrooms. Once everyone agrees on the list of choice options, they begin implementing the strategy with Charlie in their classrooms. To select choices, they do the following.

> Ms. Foster asks Charlie to have lunch with her in the cafeteria. As she enters the room and meets up with Charlie, she is friendly and professional, but thinks of the lunch as a difficult task to be gotten through. She is surprised to find the lunch and conversation with Charlie refreshing. Charlie jokes with the lunch attendants, fellow students, and the custodian. He jokes in a bighearted, generous way that makes people laugh. "You're very kind toward people, and witty!" Ms. Foster remarks.
>
> "I'm good with language, so wit comes easily to me," Charlie responds. "I like making people laugh because I can see easily how to do it, and doing it makes me feel confident and like I can use what I'm good at to accomplish something good. Things I'm not so good at are harder for me to face, especially if I have to face a lot of what I'm not good at all at once."

"Like in math class?" Ms. Foster asks.

"Yes, like in math class," Charlie says.

Later, Charlie has similar meetings with Ms. Hurst and Mr. Woodruff. In these meetings, Charlie's teachers gain insight into Charlie's mindset and some factors contributing to his disruptive behaviors in their classes. Charlie also increases his self-awareness as he talks about his likes and dislikes, and the things that are easy and more difficult for him.

After the one-to-one meetings, Ms. Hurst decides to implement choice with Charlie by allowing him the flexibility to choose the order in which he completes his work (reading, researching, or writing) during independent time. Mr. Woodruff decides to implement choice with Charlie by allowing him to choose what area in the classroom he would like to use to complete his independent classwork. Charlie may choose to complete his classwork in the leisure area with beanbags and carpet, at his desk, at the long table near Mr. Woodruff's desk, or in the private study carrel in the back of the classroom. Last, Ms. Foster gives Charlie the opportunity to choose ten out of twenty mathematics problems to solve for his daily mathematics independent work so that he doesn't feel overwhelmed by something he is struggling with.

Charlie is excited about having some control over his schoolwork. In fact, he tells Mr. Woodruff that school has actually become *enjoyable*—and not just the part of school where he makes people laugh!

As you can see, Charlie's teachers take Charlie's preferences and personal experience into account, so the choice they offer is not arbitrary; instead, it comes out of Charlie's needs and preferences and fits what is feasible within these teachers' particular classrooms and schedules. The parameters for feasibility will differ depending on the teacher, the classroom, the time frame, and, of course, the student.

It is important that students be involved in the choice-making process. When students are involved in the process, they are able to express their interests and are more likely to complete the choices, the reinforcements, or both; this, in turn, promotes appropriate behaviors and reduces challenging behaviors.

Review Ideas for Reinforcement

Providing choices needs to include positive reinforcement for completing an assigned task (Landrum & Sweigart, 2014). For example, once the student completes the choice task, the student may be reinforced with verbal praise from the teacher. Verbal praise, though an external reinforcer, will most often demonstrate respect for the student's developing internal motivation, as it specifically addresses the student's success with a choice he, she, or they helped craft and select. However, there are other extrinsic ways to reinforce a student when providing choices. Intrinsic reinforcements (that is, reinforcements that give students personal satisfaction for completing work or positive feelings for pleasing the teacher) and extrinsic reinforcements together can motivate students with challenging behaviors in completing their assigned school tasks. Teachers may reinforce students with various extrinsic reinforcers if the students find choice making unpleasant or have difficulty following through on a choice. This additional extrinsic reinforcement may motivate students with challenging behaviors to complete the choice-making activity. The concept is the students will choose the type of positive reinforcement they desire after completing a task. Positive reinforcements might include the following.

- Screen time

- Free time to read, complete outside classwork, or socialize with peers

- Recess or gym time

- Time to listen to music

- Time to work with a peer

Teachers collect data to ensure positive reinforcement with choice decreases problem behaviors. You could use the event recording or scatterplot assessment again for this data collection (pages 38–39), or you could use other tools supplied by your school district. As the student demonstrates progress, you can incorporate reinforcement in a variety of contexts as needed to continue appropriate behaviors.

In the scenario, Charlie and his teachers worked together to determine what choices he would like to receive. Each teacher and Charlie need to agree on reinforcement options as well. During all independent work, Ms. Hurst periodically reminds Charlie of the reinforcements he will earn when he successfully completes his independent work. They agreed that when Charlie completes his independent work, he can choose to listen to music on his phone, play a school-appropriate game on the computer, or talk to his friends for a short time at the end of class. Since Charlie chose his reinforcements based on his interests, he is more invested in completing his classwork with minimum challenging behaviors. Each teacher also provides specific verbal praise when Charlie completes his independent work.

EXAMPLES OF HOW TO UTILIZE CHOICE

Teachers can incorporate choice-making opportunities throughout the school day in any number of settings and scenarios (Jolivette et al., 2017). Choices should be individualized to align with the needs and preferences of individual students, and teachers can also use choices with small groups and whole classrooms. Let's take a look at some different examples of providing choices to students. The following list shares guidance, after which we will explore example elementary and secondary choice sheets.

- **People:** Allow students to decide who they will work with, who they will sit next to, and so on. For example, if students will be working in small groups, allow them some choice regarding who will be in each group (to the extent that is appropriate depending on student dynamics). Teachers can also incorporate people as a choice related to reinforcement. A student might be particularly fond of a specific teacher or paraprofessional, for example. Working toward spending time with that person at lunch, during recess, or at the end of the day can be a powerful motivator.

- **Order of work completion:** Allow students to decide the order in which they will complete the assigned work.

- **Location:** Provide students with several different options for where they will complete their work. For independent work time, students may receive the option to move to a different part of the classroom.

- **Duration:** Involve students in determining how long they will work before receiving a short break from the task, activity, or assignment.

- **Positive reinforcement:** Use student interests and preferences to generate a list of positive reinforcements. Students can choose from the list after completion of a task or assignment. Be creative when you generate the list! Consider the wide range of items or activities students ask for regularly; this is the easiest way to determine what your students find reinforcing. For example, if students are always asking for time on their tablet computers, then you know offering that time will serve as a strong reinforcer.

- **Materials:** When designing an assignment, task, or activity, think about ways in which you could vary the materials needed. For example, students could make the following choices.

  - Choose between a whiteboard and notebook paper.

- Choose the font in which you write your paper.

- Choose to use markers instead of pencils.

- Choose from a variety of subjects for a report or project.

- **Knowledge demonstration:** Students can express their acquisition of knowledge in a variety of ways. Be creative, and consider the different ways in which students can demonstrate what they have learned. Students could choose to express their knowledge via a poster presentation, a video recording, a podcast, or an oral exam. This list is not exhaustive, and we encourage you to think outside the proverbial box when giving students options.

Figure 2.3 is an example of how a choice sheet could be used in an elementary classroom. The teacher or teacher's aide presents the choice sheet to the student needing supplemental support, and the student chooses the preferred activity (by either verbally communicating the choice or marking it). The student then immediately receives access to that activity or is told when the activity will be available.

Name: Abby   **Date:** 10/6

Directions:

1. Circle the activity you would like to work on.

2. Complete the activity.

3. After completing the activity, make a mark through it on the choice board, and select another activity.

4. Continue selecting and completing activities until you have completed at least six activities.

Dinosaur Unit Choice Sheet

Dinosaur Books	Dinosaur Puzzles	Online Dinosaur Games
Dinosaur Adding and Subtracting	Ten-Minute Break	Snack
Dinosaur Arts and Crafts	Dinosaur Board Games	Dinosaur Writing

---

Figure 2.3: Dinosaur unit choice sheet.

Visit **go.SolutionTree.com/behavior** *for a free reproducible version of this figure.*

Figure 2.4 provides an example of how a choice sheet could be used in a secondary classroom. The teacher provides the sheet to students, and the students decide the order in which they will complete the work.

Name: Marcus   **Date:** 2/10

All items are due on Friday. After you complete each item, let me know so that I can initial your form. Be prepared to show proof that you have completed the item. Remember, your end-of-unit project is due on April 9!

Algebra 2 Choice Sheet

Completion of Guided Notes	Word Problems 1–10	Calculation Problems 1–20
Weekly Partner Work	Five Minutes of Free Time	End-of-Week Test
Word Problems 11–20	Calculation Problems 21–40	Work on End-of-Unit Project
Online Mathematics Games (Twenty minutes)	Homework Corrections	Five Minutes of Free Time

---

Figure 2.4: Algebra 2 choice sheet.

Visit go.SolutionTree.com/behavior for a free reproducible version of this figure.

Teachers should collect data the entire time they are implementing the choice strategy because data will show whether the strategy is working. You may need to make adjustments to ensure success. For example, the choice or reinforcement options may need to be adjusted. It is also a good idea to reflect to ensure you are correctly implementing the strategy. Talking with the students about how they feel things are going is important too. Teachers should always be asking themselves about why a student displays challenging behaviors as well, as emphasized in chapter 1 (page 5), to help ensure they are meeting the needs of the student.

After six weeks of providing Charlie with choices, his three teachers meet to discuss the results from their data collection (for example, data collection forms, observation data, and independent classwork completion). Unsurprisingly, Ms. Hurst's data reveal that in her class, Charlie has the fewest challenging behaviors when asked to complete his independent work. Since Charlie enjoys social studies—and more specifically, his independent writing assignments—more than science and mathematics, he often chooses to complete his writing assignments before his research and reading assignments. In addition, his reinforcements (for example, computer time and socialization with friends for five minutes at the end of class) further inspire him to finish his work peacefully.

Ms. Foster, Charlie's mathematics teacher, sees Charlie exhibit the most challenging behaviors (for example, refusal to complete classwork and verbal aggression) in her subject, but the data reveal a slight decrease in his challenging behaviors. Ms. Foster allowed Charlie to choose ten of the twenty mathematics problems to complete for his independent work. Ms. Foster explains that Charlie would often complain and pout about the work when she assigned it to him. In these cases, she would quickly discuss the reinforcements he was earning and the modified independent work he needed to complete. Ms. Foster states that Charlie's attitude became more positive after these discussions. She also states she purposely ignored his persistent complaining on a few occasions. Charlie did complete all his modified mathematics assignments during this six-week intervention. Before she implemented this secondary tier intervention, Charlie would refuse to complete his independent mathematics classwork on a weekly basis. Ms. Foster will continue to collect data on utilizing choice with Charlie and reconvene with the team to discuss his progress at the end of the next six-week period.

Finally, Mr. Woodruff reports that Charlie maintained his challenging behaviors in science. When Mr. Woodruff offered Charlie his independent work, he allowed Charlie to choose the location where he wanted to complete this assignment (that is, the leisure area with beanbags and carpet, his desk, the long table near Mr. Woodruff's desk, or the private study carrel in the back of the classroom). Upon review of his data collection sheets and observation notes, Mr. Woodruff confirms that Charlie wasted an immense amount of time deciding where he wanted to complete his independent assignments. The team concludes that Charlie has too many choices in this case and advises Mr. Woodruff to give Charlie only two choices of where to complete his independent work in his classroom. Furthermore, Charlie earned a small amount of computer time in Mr. Woodruff's classroom as his positive reinforcement, and Charlie mentioned, on several occasions throughout the six weeks, that Mr. Woodruff's computer games were boring and outdated. Ms. Hurst and Ms. Foster discuss this with Mr. Woodruff, and Mr. Woodruff opts to use the same games in his classroom as they do. Mr. Woodruff will revise his providing-choice intervention and reinforcements, discuss them with Charlie, and begin collecting data. The team will meet in another six weeks to discuss the progress of providing Charlie with choices in Mr. Woodruff's science class.

In our example, you see the importance of data collection. Because Charlie's teachers regularly collected data in this scenario, they were able to adjust the plan to ensure Charlie's success. When you regularly collect data, you can have a true picture of what is happening and can make adjustments as needed. You don't want to try the strategy for a day or two and then stop implementing it altogether if you feel it is not working. Data collection will help you better understand why the strategy is working in some instances and not in others. From there, you can adjust. Continued data collection will then help you know the adjustments were effective if the desired behaviors increase and the challenging behaviors decrease.

In table 2.3, we provide you with a short list of dos and don'ts for implementing choice in the classroom.

Table 2.3: Dos and Don'ts for Providing Choices

Do	Don't
✓ Draw on students' strengths and interests.	✗ Conceptualize providing choices as giving your students anything they want.
✓ Involve your students in developing your process for providing different choices.	✗ Lower your standards in the choices you provide for your students.
✓ Make sure you collect data to see what is effective.	✗ Argue or bargain with students over choices to make.
✓ Provide choices before the assigned task begins.	✗ Provide choices during the task when emotions are heightened to avoid conflict.
✓ Get to know your student to learn about the student's preferences.	✗ Create a plan without talking to the student and others who work with the student.
✓ Rely on data to inform decisions about what is working and what isn't working.	✗ Provide choice options or reinforcement inconsistently.
✓ Remember that consistency is key.	✗ Threaten or yell at the student.

CONCLUDING THOUGHTS

Choice is a relatively easy evidence-based strategy to implement. What is great about choice is it can benefit all students in the classroom but can be specifically tailored for students with challenging behaviors. It is a tier 1 preventive and proactive strategy. Teachers need to make sure they are implementing choice in a way that matches the why of students' challenging behaviors from chapter 1 (page 5).

Remember, when implementing choice, to consider the student's cultural and linguistic background. Involving the student in the process will help you ensure you are not only meeting the student's cultural and linguistic needs but also tailoring choice options and reinforcement options to the student's needs. Data collection must be part of the entire process so you know whether the choice is working and whether adjustments need to be made.

Next, we provide reflective questions to ask yourself as you are implementing choice. In the appendix (page 165), we have provided resources you can consult as you implement the choice strategy.

Chapter 2: Questions for Reflection

Write your responses to the following questions. Keep these responses in mind as you work to address challenging student behaviors and guide your students toward academic engagement and motivated learning.

1. Can you see yourself providing more choices in a structured manner within your classroom? Why or why not?

2. Describe what you believe the biggest obstacles could be when implementing the choice strategy with your students. What could you do to overcome the obstacles?

3. Describe what you believe the biggest benefits could be when implementing the choice strategy with your students.

4. Think about a student you currently work with who you believe might benefit from the choice strategy. What steps would you need to take to implement this evidence-based practice based on what you learned from the chapter?

Motivated to Learn © 2023 Solution Tree Press • SolutionTree.com
Visit **go.SolutionTree.com/behavior** to download this free reproducible.

5. What are some reinforcers that you think your students would be interested in? Think about reinforcers that don't cost money (for example, privilege passes) and some low-cost items students might enjoy.

6. What are some different activities that you include in a choice sheet for your students?

7. Describe the system you have for getting to know your students' families and communicating with them.

8. After implementing choice in your classroom, answer this question: "What went well?"

9. Did you have any challenges implementing choice in your classroom? If so, what were they? What adjustments could make choice work better for you?

10. Reflect on the choices you offered. Are there more choices you'd like to add? Are there choices you offered that you might not include again?

Chapter 3

It's All About the Reward: A Guide to Token Economies

Since Nichols Elementary School implemented its schoolwide PBIS framework, one specific evidence-based practice that has been successful with the student body is the token-economy system. The students take pride in earning tokens as accolades for their positive behaviors. The school affectionately calls their tokens, large paper circles labeled with the school's name, *Nichols nickels*. An image of a Nichols nickel appears in figure 3.1.

Figure 3.1: Nichols nickel.

Ms. Bogie and Mr. McCurley are both fourth-grade teachers at Nichols Elementary School. Ms. Bogie is a general education teacher of twenty-three years and is known among the students for her stern demeanor. During the schoolwide professional learning on PBIS, Ms. Bogie did not seem to buy into the principles of PBIS. She believes students should "just act right," and her disciplinary techniques are considered old-fashioned. Mr. McCurley is also a general education teacher and has worked at Nichols Elementary for twelve years. Students are fond of Mr. McCurley's positive energy. He enjoyed learning about PBIS during the training and even volunteered to work on the school's PBIS committee to learn more about effective practices of the framework. Ms. Bogie and Mr. McCurley manage their classrooms very differently. Specifically, Ms. Bogie has a reactive zero-tolerance policy, while Mr. McCurley is more proactive and preventive.

A student, Jeffery, is currently repeating the fourth grade and has experienced both these teachers' classroom management styles. Jeffery enjoys science and being with his friends. His favorite subject in school is physical education because of his love of basketball. When he is on the basketball court with his peers, he is always the tallest kid and the most dedicated to scoring points. School staff describe Jeffery as a bright kid who often lets his lack of motivation and lack of pride in his classwork hinder his ability to be successful in school.

During his first year in fourth grade, Jeffery often refused to complete his schoolwork for his teacher, Ms. Bogie. He would sit at his desk fidgeting with paper clips, digging in his book bag, and using any other materials he could find to divert his attention from completing his work. He would also try to disturb other students in class. Jeffery and Ms. Bogie's relationship was tense. He was in trouble most of the time.

For his second year in fourth grade, Jeffery has been placed with Mr. McCurley, who adopted most aspects of the school's token-economy system for his own classwide token-economy system. Through his system, Mr. McCurley's students can earn Nichols nickels for exhibiting appropriate classroom behavior, such as completing assignments in a timely manner, participating in class discussion, following the classroom rules, and helping peers when needed. Jeffery and his classmates earn these reinforcers multiple times a day.

Every Friday, which the students affectionately call *Fun Friday*, the students can cash in their Nichols nickels at the school store for their tangible reinforcements. Mr. McCurley's students can also choose to cash in their Nichols nickels on Friday mornings within the class gift store. The reinforcements in Mr. McCurley's class store are intentionally different from those in the school store.

A *token economy* is a reinforcement system used to decrease problem behaviors and increase desirable behaviors. The token-economy system has been well established in the literature and widely used to reduce challenging behaviors (Ivy, Meindl, Overley, & Robson, 2017).

In the scenario described here, stakeholders at Nichols Elementary School (teachers, paraprofessionals, principals, bus drivers, cafeteria workers, and so on) receive professional learning on the importance of distributing Nichols nickels as reinforcers when students exhibit positive behaviors within the school's mission. This professional development also trains stakeholders to describe *why* the students are earning the Nichols nickels. Students, like Jeffery and his peers, earn tokens (tangible or intangible) when they demonstrate desirable behaviors; they can exchange the tokens for various items (for example, privileges and prizes).

The token-economy system is easily customizable and implemented schoolwide, classwide, or individually, and it can be used with students at both the elementary and secondary levels. As soon as students engage in the desired behavior, they receive immediate feedback and earn the token with specific praise. Token economies promote on-task behavior, class participation, and task completion, which promote a more positive learning environment and higher student achievement (Ackerman, Samudre, & Allday, 2020).

This chapter makes clear how to develop and customize a token-economy system for either an individual or a group, such as a whole class. The chapter leads you through how token-economy systems work, how an appreciation for students' cultural and linguistic diversity should inform the design of the token-economy system, and the role student interest should play in the design. It also covers how to teach students to use the system and how to extend the system's impact with reinforcements. The chapter wraps up with a Concluding Thoughts section and a reproducible page that includes reflective questions to ponder. The chapter will revisit the Jeffery and Mr. McCurley scenario throughout to make the concepts of the chapter visible within an imaginary school context.

HOW TO IMPLEMENT A TOKEN ECONOMY

A token economy can be a tier 1 or tier 2 strategy. In the sections that follow, we go into detail about how a token economy can be utilized schoolwide, classwide, and individually. Much like choice, a token economy requires considering students' interests. If students are not interested in the options provided, they are less likely to do what you want them to do as you are implementing a token economy. You must teach students how the token economy works because if they don't understand your expectations, they are less likely to be successful. Additionally, you should reinforce students for following your expectations because, as we presented in chapter 1 (page 5), research supports positive reinforcement over punitive measures.

Effectively implementing a token-economy system involves taking some important steps (Ivy et al., 2017). Following are the five steps for developing a token-economy system.

1. **Determine the components of schoolwide, classwide, and individualized token-economy systems:** Determining the components requires considering the scale of the token-economy system, the types of tokens to be used, how tokens will be exchanged, what challenging behaviors the token-economy system will target, and more. This section provides guidance on these considerations to aid effective implementation of the system.

2. **Consider cultural and linguistic diversity:** It is critically important to be aware of your own biases as an educator—and the ways your students' cultural and linguistic background influences what is considered normal behavior for them—when implementing a behavioral modification system with an individual, class, or school. This section helps educators do just that in preparation for implementing the token-economy system.

3. **Incorporate student interests in implementation:** If the token-economy system does not respond to students' actual interests, it will not be effective. This section guides educators through strategies to learn student interests, such as student interest surveys and one-to-one conversations.

4. **Teach the token-economy system:** Educators must provide explicit descriptions of how the token-economy system works and role-play with students to learn the system. This section covers these vital teaching steps.

5. **Review ideas for reinforcement:** This section guides educators in effectively using extrinsic motivators to extend the impact of the token-economy system. Educators work toward the long-term goal of helping students develop the intrinsic motivation that will lead them to academic and personal success.

Determine the Components of Schoolwide, Classwide, and Individualized Token-Economy Systems

A schoolwide system is a proactive and preventive way to support all students. In this case, the entire school uses the same system as we describe. If your school does not have a schoolwide system, you can implement a classwide system. To do this, you first need a plan for implementation (Scott, 2017). Consider specifically, What behaviors will earn tokens? What type of tokens will you use? How and when will students exchange tokens? For schoolwide or classwide token-economy systems, will your students receive tangible tokens or tickets, or will you use an electronic-based system, such as ClassDojo (https://classdojo.com), where students receive virtual tokens? If you decide to use tangible tokens, we recommend having a place where students put them to prevent off-task behavior during instructional time (for example, fidgeting with the tokens). You can tailor the tokens, tickets, or electronic system to students at the elementary and secondary levels. Schoolwide and classwide token-economy systems are beneficial as motivation for the whole group, whereas individualized token-economy systems can increase motivation in one student.

In schoolwide and classwide token-economy systems, teachers reinforce students with tickets or virtual tickets when they see them doing things that have been stated and taught as the expectations in the classroom. For example, when you see a student or a class sitting quietly, you can give the students tickets. Rather than pointing out every time students are not following directions, you are pointing out *when* students are following directions. The more positives you point out, the more positives you will see.

Students can cash in their tickets for various items. Items may include privilege passes (such as lunch-with-a-friend passes, homework passes, sit-in-a-special-chair passes, no-shoes passes, or free 100 percent passes) or items for cost (such as soda passes, pencils, pens, or vending-machine passes). Items students purchase can cost different amounts. For example, pizza with the principal or teacher will cost much more than a pencil or a pen.

As we noted in chapter 1 (page 5), most students will respond to tier 1 preventive and proactive approaches like the token economy. However, you may have students who need additional support. You can use an individualized token economy for students who need the additional support. These students can still earn tickets or tokens at tier 1, but will also have an individualized system under tier 2. We will spend the rest of the chapter focusing on students with challenging behaviors who need additional support at tier 2.

For an individualized token-economy system, teachers can create a token-economy sheet based on the needs of a particular student exhibiting challenging behaviors. They can use tally marks, stickers, or smiley faces to denote successes. Because the token-economy system can be individualized, teachers can easily tailor it to elementary *and* secondary students. For example, students at the elementary level may want stickers or smiley faces, while students at the secondary level will probably prefer check marks or plus signs. It is important to consider the student's interests when creating an individualized system. Later in this chapter, we will talk further about making sure a token-economy system is based on students' interests and considers their cultural and linguistic needs.

Next, we share examples of recording sheets the teachers use with students. Some students with challenging behaviors need something tangible and direct they can hold on to, like an individualized recording sheet. When the recording sheet is tailored to a specific student, it becomes more meaningful. You may render the recording sheet examples as physical copies that can be placed in a folder or on a clipboard the students carry throughout the day. You can complete an electronic copy for individuals who prefer using technology over having hard copies of recording sheets.

In figure 3.2, the teacher circles a plus sign each time the desired behaviors occur. Or, rather than having the plus signs already added, the teacher can leave the points section blank and add a sticker, smiley face, or check mark each time a desired behavior occurs. Classroom teachers or paraprofessionals are the individuals who would add these components to the recording sheets. At the end of the day, the student and teacher discuss and document something good that happened during the day and also discuss whether the student has something to work on for the next day. Students then write these things in their own words on the recording sheet.

Name: Maddy	Date: 5/8	
Target Behaviors	**Points**	**Total**
Following directions	⊕ ⊕ ⊕ ⊕ ⊕ ⊕ + + + +	6
Keeping hands and feet to self	⊕ ⊕ ⊕ ⊕ + + + + + +	4
Using kind words	⊕ ⊕ ⊕ ⊕ ⊕ ⊕ ⊕ ⊕ ⊕ +	9

Today, something positive I did was that I used kind words 9 out of 10 times today. I want to work on following directions and keeping my hands and feet to myself.

Figure 3.2: Example token-economy recording sheet.

Visit go.SolutionTree.com/behavior for a free reproducible version of this figure.

An individualized token-economy system is beneficial in that the student with challenging behaviors receives frequent feedback from this tier 2 intervention. However, it can be time-consuming for the teacher to mark every occurrence of the target behaviors. Rather than receiving a mark for every occurrence of the desired behaviors, students may receive a smiley face, sticker, or tally mark from the teacher during *each block of time* the target behaviors occur. If the desired behaviors do not occur within the time block, then the teacher can add an *X*, dash, or sad face. We recommend adding some type of mark rather than leaving the space blank to ensure you do not forget the space. Although students do not receive immediate feedback each time the desired behavior occurs, this version of a token economy is less time intensive.

In our example scenario, Mr. McCurley is using a classwide token-economy system. The class can earn Nichols nickels for following the class rules. Students can exchange the tokens they have earned on Fridays. Mr. McCurley also has a more individualized system specifically for Jeffery. Figure 3.3 shows an example of Jeffery's individual token-economy sheet on one day. He is working on following directions, keeping his hands and feet to himself, and completing assigned tasks. Each smiley face Jeffery earns is equal to one token that he can exchange at the end of each day if he so chooses. If Jeffery were a secondary student, Mr. McCurley could use plus and minus signs or check marks and Xs, rather than the smiley faces and Xs being used.

Name: Jeffery   **Date: 4/27**

TIME	Following Directions	Keeping Hands and Feet to Self	Completing Assigned Tasks
8:00–9:00 a.m.	☺	☺	☺
9:00–10:00 a.m.	☺	☺	X
10:00–11:00 a.m.	☺	☺	☺
11:00 a.m.–12:00 p.m.	X	☺	☺
12:00–1:00 p.m.	☺	X	☺
1:00–2:00 p.m.	☺	☺	☺
2:00–3:00 p.m.	☺	X	☺

Today, something positive I did was:
I got all smiley faces during three blocks of time!

I want to work on:
Completing my assigned work

Figure 3.3: Jeffery's token-economy recording sheet.

*Visit **go.SolutionTree.com/behavior** for a free reproducible version of this figure.*

In our example, Jeffery earned seventeen smiley faces!

In a classwide system, there can be a time of the day or a day of the week to exchange tokens for a reinforcer (for example, a homework pass). When you implement token economies individually, it is best to start out with a daily exchange and make adjustments as the student begins to demonstrate the desired behavior more often. For some students, an exchange before lunch may be necessary, and the exchange can then slowly fade to the end of the day as behaviors improve.

Consider Cultural and Linguistic Diversity

It is crucial to be aware of how your own expectations as an educator inform what you assume about your students. You need to remember that behavioral norms and expectations are different among cultures when considering what behaviors to target with a token-economy system, for instance. Behaviors that are considered acceptable within your students' cultural norms may differ from what you consider acceptable and *want* them to demonstrate. Educators must consciously work to make sure their biases do not unintentionally interfere with their ability to support their students. With this in mind, let's take a look at the demographic differences between teachers and students in schools in the United States.

- **Teacher demographics in U.S. schools, 2017–2018:** The following percentages represent federal data on the self-reported race and ethnicity of K–12 public school teachers in the United States (Taie & Goldring, 2020).

    ‣ American Indian or Alaska Native—0.5 percent

    ‣ Asian—2.2 percent

    ‣ Black—6.3 percent

    ‣ Latinx—9.1 percent

    ‣ Native Hawaiian or Pacific Islander—0.2 percent

    ‣ Two or more races—1.7 percent

    ‣ White—80 percent

- **Student demographics in U.S. schools, 2017–2018:** The following percentages represent federal data on the race and ethnicity of students in U.S. K–12 public schools as reported by their parents or guardians. (Note from source [National Center for Education Statistics, 2020]: "Detail may not sum to totals because of rounding. Although rounded numbers are displayed, the figures are based on unrounded data.")

- American Indian or Alaska Native—1 percent
- Asian—5 percent
- Black—15 percent
- Latinx—28 percent
- Native Hawaiian or Pacific Islander—<1 percent
- Two or more races—5 percent
- White—46 percent

Considering the cultural differences present in classrooms, teachers should do the following important things to make token economies culturally responsive. Keep these things in mind.

- Use your students' preferred language when posting instructions related to the token economy, including the expected behaviors, item choices, and so on.

- Be cognizant of the role your own belief system has in determining behaviors to target for change (LeBlanc, 2016). The article "A Conceptual Framework for Creating Culturally Responsive Token Economies" (LeBlanc, 2016) includes several powerful anecdotes about how teachers' best intentions can sometimes be misguided. For example, a teacher recounts how male students in one school were fined class currency they had earned for *flexing* or attempting to intimidate their peers by standing over one another. One day, a teacher overheard a father informing his son that he had to walk home alone that afternoon and to walk "hard" as a form of self-protection when he got to a notoriously dangerous street. That father-son conversation led the teacher to revamp his approach. He taught students the behaviors he did want to see in his classroom instead of penalizing them for behaviors he did not want the students to demonstrate (LeBlanc, 2016).

- Communicate with your students' families about the token-economy system. If the family members speak a language other than English, make sure your correspondence is translated as needed. There are free websites that can help with this. In your communication (for example, hard copies of a class newsletter, emails, and the class website), include the following.

  - A brief overview of the system
  - Behaviors that you are striving to promote among the students

- ‣ Examples, and corresponding prices, of items that the students can purchase with the tokens

- Create a system that encourages a sense of community in the classroom. Involve your students in creating the currency or tokens, items to be purchased, and so on.

- Create a system that supports student engagement in the classroom. Consider how students can earn tokens through teamwork, productive group work, participation, intervention when they witness bullying, and so on.

Incorporate Student Interests in Implementation

Prior to implementing the token-economy system, teachers must involve students in the process in order to learn about reinforcers students are interested in earning. Having the entire class fill out an interest survey is always a great way to learn about all your students' interests, which is important. If you have an individualized token economy for a student with challenging behaviors, you can revisit the interest survey or have a one-to-one conversation with the student to learn more about the student's interests as they specifically relate to the token-economy system. Having a one-to-one conversation with the student is a great opportunity for a positive interaction that focuses on answering, "How can I help you be successful?" rather than on pointing out negative behaviors the student has, which is often what students with challenging behaviors experience. The one-to-one conversation can include finding out what behavior-tracking method the student prefers (for example, smiley and frowny faces, plus and minus signs, or Xs and Os) and what incentives the student wants to earn. If students are not interested in the reinforcements they can earn, they are less likely to engage in the desired appropriate behaviors.

To help prevent satiation (that is, decreased effectiveness due to overuse of the same reinforcers), create a menu of reinforcers everyone has agreed on based on students' interests (Ackerman et al., 2020). The students should also help decide when they will check in with you to cash in tokens for reinforcements. Some students may need to do this two times a day, such as before lunch and at the end of the day. Other students can cash in at the end of the day. The more involved the student is in planning an individualized token economy, the more ownership the student will have, and the more likely that student will be to succeed. It is important to note that younger students (particularly those in kindergarten) will need more guidance when making implementation decisions than older students will. However, students at all ages can provide valuable information teachers can use when making implementation decisions.

Once you have gotten as much input as you can from the student to incorporate his, her, or their interests, you can create a menu based on this input. The menu can be electronic, typed, or written on paper. The menu can be in a list format if the reinforcements don't have a price. However, if the student will earn different incentives based on different cash-in amounts, then you can create a menu based on price. The menu should provide enough choices so the student has options to choose from. The menu can easily be tailored for elementary students (fidget toys, candy, pencils) and secondary students (free dress day, homework pass, vending-machine pass) because the menu is specific to the students' interests.

Jeffery and Mr. McCurley, for example, created the following reinforcement menu based on Jeffery's interests; the items Jeffery can earn have different values associated with them. Although the menu that follows is tailored for Jeffery, who is in elementary school, it can easily be tailored to meet the needs of a student at the secondary level. Maybe instead of computer time, although secondary students enjoy this, it could include cell phone time. Students at the secondary level may also really enjoy a homework pass or a snack-machine pass. Some secondary schools have assigned seating at lunch, but other schools don't, so lunch with a buddy may not apply. However, lunch with a buddy outside may work. Some students at the secondary level may enjoy lunch with a teacher. Rather than a whoopsie pass, the secondary-level list may include a free 100 percent on a daily assignment. Any reinforcement menu list must incorporate a student's interests to be meaningful for the student, which will ultimately help ensure the token-economy system created is successful.

- Ten minutes of computer time (ten Nichols nickels)
- Homework pass (fifteen Nichols nickels)
- Snack-machine pass (twenty Nichols nickels)
- Lunch with a buddy (twenty-five Nichols nickels)
- Lunch with Mr. McCurley (thirty Nichols nickels)
- Whoopsie pass (thirty-five Nichols nickels)

Mr. McCurley and Jeffery agreed to meet again six weeks after implementing the token-economy system to discuss and determine whether the menu needed to change.

Teach the Token-Economy System

Students need explicit examples of how to earn tokens and how and when to spend them. Role-playing various situations can help students practice what it looks like to earn tickets or tokens. The teacher might state the expectations, model the expected behavior, and then explain what will happen when the behavior is displayed. For example, before it's time to get in line, the teacher can explain how this is done and can even have a student model it. The student then receives the ticket or token. The teacher can then have a small group try, and as the students are getting in the line, the teacher can say, "Wow! Look at this group getting in line by walking and keeping their hands to themselves. That is awesome! Here is a ticket for each of you!" At the secondary level, the students can practice leaving the classroom after the teacher dismisses them, whether or not the bell to move to the next class has rung. The teacher first explains what is going to happen, how it will happen, and what happens when directions are followed.

At the school level, details on how the system works should be sent to parents, guardians, and caregivers. The teacher should also explain the system in the classroom. The principal can explain and reinforce it during a pep rally too. The details of how the system works should be posted throughout the school. A classwide system operates much like a schoolwide system. The teacher sends a note home about how the system works and posts details of how the system works in the classroom. However, students receive a copy to put in a binder or folder. The reinforcement menu with prices included should also be posted for students to view at all levels.

Review Ideas for Reinforcement

Token economies cannot function adequately without reinforcements. The ultimate goal of all reinforcement is to arrive at a place where the student no longer needs additional resources—where the student acts within a naturalistic environment and no longer works for tokens but instead works for verbal praise or the intrinsic reinforcement (feeling proud of oneself for doing a good job) that comes from completing a task (Scheuermann & Hall, 2016). The teacher monitors students' points to determine whether the system is working and whether adjustments need to be made.

Fading the tokens to be given less frequently occurs as target behaviors consistently improve. The student will no longer need the individualized system at tier 2 and moves to tier 1 to receive the same preventive and proactive system as the rest of the students. However, note that some students may prefer to continue using the individualized system because they recognize it helps them be successful. If this is the case, the students may decide they don't need the individualized reinforcements daily and choose instead to cash in one time per week. Talk with the students to learn what they feel is best for themselves to have success. Having a conversation about fading the token-economy system can be exciting for the student and the teacher because it is a time of completely positive talk about how successful the student has been. The teacher and student can discuss how proud they are of how hard the student has been working.

Let's revisit the scenario with Mr. McCurley and Jeffery to see how Jeffery's intrinsic motivation has grown through his use of an individualized token-economy system.

> Mr. McCurley and Jeffery meet to discuss how things are going. They look over Jeffery's token-economy recording sheets and see Jeffery is doing really well. His challenging behaviors are decreasing, and his positive behaviors are increasing. "I'm so proud of you!" Mr. McCurley tells Jeffery. "Are you proud of yourself too?" Jeffery explains to Mr. McCurley that he feels proud of himself and also says that he is excited he has been receiving Bs and Cs on his assignments.
>
> Mr. McCurley asks Jeffery if he likes the incentives he has been earning from his reinforcement menu. Jeffery asks if they could add receiving candy (Hot Tamales) and playing a card game with a friend to the list. They decide that the candy will be worth twenty smiley faces, and the card game with a buddy will be worth twenty-five smiley faces. Jeffery also asks if maybe everything could cost more smiley faces. "I want to challenge myself a little bit," he says. He and Mr. McCurley raise the price of everything by five tokens. Jeffery has been cashing in daily, but he and Mr. McCurley decide he can wait a few days. They also decide to check in every day and talk about how things are going. Mr. McCurley challenges Jeffery (with a smile on his face) to see if he can wait until Friday to cash in. Mr. McCurley tells Jeffery he thinks he can do it because he's been so successful so far. Jeffery feels like he is up for the challenge!

Reading about Jeffery's newfound intrinsic motivation, you may think it seems impossible. However, fading does happen naturally. Many students are successful and don't need an individualized system any longer. Students with challenging behaviors begin to feel proud of themselves because they are succeeding academically and behaviorally and, in turn, are earning the positive reinforcement at a much higher rate. Students are able to be successful with just the schoolwide or classwide systems that are always there and often reach the point where they don't need the specific individualized system anymore.

When reinforcements are used, however, the classroom teachers and administrators should distribute and post reinforcement menus for the student body on the first day of school and gather information from the students about what reinforcements they would like to earn in the school or classroom store. Following are examples of schoolwide and classroom reinforcements to use with a token economy.

For schoolwide and classroom incentives, students enjoy buying trinkets, books, and toys. The ideas provided in the following lists can apply for individual students as well. It all goes back to finding reinforcement ideas that match the interests of the students they are for. Some students may also enjoy purchasing personal hygiene items to keep in their lockers at school. In addition, when a holiday is approaching (for example, Mother's Day), they enjoy buying gifts for their loved ones from the school store.

- **Elementary menu examples:** Students at the elementary level may prefer a combination of privileges and trinkets for their reinforcements. Learn the interests of your students to determine what reinforcements they like. For example, is there a particular type of pencil or small toy students like, or do they have a favorite type of candy? Students may fill out an interest survey, which they can complete in the classroom or at home and take back to school. Interests could also be part of a class discussion. It is important to note that students who have moved to tier 2 may also like items from the list provided. This list simply features ideas that any student at the elementary level may enjoy.

  ‣ Fidget toys or other small toys

  ‣ Pencils

  ‣ Stickers

  ‣ Whoopsie pass

  ‣ Piece of candy

  ‣ Lunch with a friend

  ‣ Lunch with the teacher

  ‣ Computer time

  ‣ Special chair

  ‣ Coupon for free time to read, complete outside classwork, or rest

  ‣ Option to move their desk for the day

  ‣ Coupon for free time to socialize with peers

  ‣ Coupon for additional recess or gym time on Friday

  ‣ Game play with the class

  ‣ Game play with a friend

  ‣ Time listening to music

  ‣ Time to complete classwork with a peer

  ‣ Educational materials or specialized writing materials (for example, mechanical pencils or decorative notebooks)

- Gifts for teachers, parents, guardians, friends, or siblings
- Books
- Class pizza party
- Class field day

- **Secondary menu examples:** Students at the secondary level often prefer reinforcements that include privileges and independence, such as the following. The teacher in students' first period or advisory class can ask students about their preference for incentives. It is important to note that just like at the elementary level, students at the secondary level who have moved to tier 2 may also like items from the list provided. This list simply features ideas that any student at the secondary level may enjoy.

  - Homework pass
  - Ten points on an assignment
  - Drink- or snack-machine pass
  - Free dress day (for schools with a dress code)
  - Lunch outside
  - Late-work pass
  - Teacher's chair
  - Electronics pass
  - Pick-music-in-the-class pass
  - Special parking space (for students who drive)
  - Option to move their desk for the day
  - Coupon for free time to socialize with peers
  - Dropped lowest grade
  - Time listening to music
  - Game play with the class
  - Game play with a friend
  - Candy bar
  - Personal hygiene items (for example, hair clips or electric toothbrushes)
  - Educational materials or specialized writing materials (for example, mechanical pencils or decorative notebooks)

- Gifts for teachers, parents, guardians, friends, or siblings
- Books

The items in both the elementary and secondary lists are just possibilities. Your students may have ideas to add that aren't on either list!

EXAMPLES OF HOW TO UTILIZE A TOKEN ECONOMY

Something we love about token economies is that you can use them in a variety of ways. Table 3.1 includes some ideas. This list is not comprehensive. Get creative and do what you feel will work best with your students.

Table 3.1: Examples of How to Utilize a Token Economy

End-of-Week Store	Students shop for just-for-fun items at the end of the week.
School Supplies	Students purchase supplemental school supplies. We do not support students having to pay for required or necessary school supplies and materials.
Fun Friday	Students can purchase thirty minutes of computer time, game time, or time sitting with friends for Friday.
Schoolwork-Related Reward	Students can purchase: • An extended due date on a project or assignment • The option to skip a night of homework
Points Spreadsheet	Secondary students utilize an electronic or hard copy of a chart that delineates the points they earn and spend. The student is responsible for keeping track of the points.
"I Am Working for . . ." Chart	Elementary students or students with cognitive issues may prefer the following chart specifics. • An image depicts a much-enjoyed activity or item. • Underneath the image, three to five blank spaces appear. • Each time the student demonstrates the desired behavior, the teacher marks one of the blanks with a smiley face, a sticker, or another appealing image. • Once all the blank spaces are filled in, the student immediately receives access to the enjoyed activity or item.

Raffle Tickets	You can distribute tickets to support desired behavior. We support not taking tickets away once the students have earned them. Doing so can unintentionally escalate challenging behavior. • Each time a student demonstrates a desired behavior, you give a raffle ticket to the student. • Instead of spending them, students keep their raffle tickets, and a prize raffle is held at the end of the week.

Now that we have gone through the steps for effectively implementing a token economy, we should refer to our scenario to see how Jeffery is doing. Specifically, has the token economy helped his positive behaviors increase and his challenging behaviors decrease?

Jeffery has been more successful during his second time in fourth grade. Mr. McCurley was able to obtain baseline data on Jeffery's behavior by using a classroom observation checklist and scatterplot data collection sheet. Data show Jeffery is being less distracting to his peers and is completing his schoolwork with minimal prompting in comparison to his first time in fourth grade. The number of smiley faces on his token-economy sheets has increased substantially. Jeffery often discusses the token economy with Mr. McCurley. Mr. McCurley welcomes these conversations and frequently praises Jeffery for his hard work in his classroom. Jeffery displays, with pride, his earned Nichols nickels in a pouch on the outside of his desk. He also always has a countdown of the days of the week until Fun Friday, when he will visit the class or school store. He usually spends his nickels on extra basketball time in the gym.

One Friday in October, Jeffery, having saved his Nichols nickels for two weeks, purchases a coffee cup that says "#1 Teacher" and gifts it to Mr. McCurley. McCurley and other stakeholders agree that Jeffery's class participation, pride in his schoolwork, and completion of assignments have increased exponentially during his second chance at fourth grade due to his investment in the token-economy system.

In table 3.2 (page 72), we provide you with a short list of dos and don'ts for implementing a token economy in the classroom. Be sure to refer to the dos and don'ts as important reminders for how to implement the token-economy strategy.

Table 3.2: Dos and Don'ts for a Token Economy

Do	Don't
✓ Deliver tokens consistently. ✓ Clearly explain the behaviors that will result in tokens. ✓ Clearly post how much items cost. ✓ Inform students of any changes you make to the system. ✓ Solicit student feedback on items to include for purchase. ✓ Keep it simple. ✓ Consider free items that reinforce your students. (Free items may include privilege passes like a homework pass, a special seat pass, or a free 100 percent pass.)	✗ Take tokens away from students for misbehavior. ✗ Inconsistently implement the token economy. ✗ Create the plan without input from the students. ✗ Begin implementing a token economy without a plan and input from all stakeholders (including the students). ✗ Use the token economy as a punishment. ✗ Develop a confusing, elaborate, or complicated system. ✗ Spend a lot of money buying tangible reinforcers.

CONCLUDING THOUGHTS

The evidence-based token-economy strategy can be implemented as a prevention strategy at tier 1, but it can also be effectively utilized as an intervention strategy at tier 2. Much as with providing choice, data should help drive the implementation of a token economy. Continually collecting and looking at data will help teachers understand what is working and what they need to adjust. While you are looking at the data, you are also determining the why of students' behavior, as you learned in chapter 1 (page 5). You need to continually seek to understand students' needs so you can ensure you are actually meeting their needs. You will better understand your students when you involve them in the process and learn their interests while considering any cultural or linguistic preferences. Doing so will allow your students with challenging behaviors to be much more successful, behaviorally and academically.

Next, we provide reflective questions to ask yourself as you are implementing a token economy. In the appendix (page 165), we have provided resources you can consult as you implement the token-economy strategy.

Chapter 3: Questions for Reflection

Write your responses to the following questions. Keep these responses in mind as you work to address challenging student behaviors and guide your students toward academic engagement and motivated learning.

1. Can you see yourself creating a token economy within your classroom? Why or why not?

   YES- IF IT IS SIMPLE (EASY TO KEEP UP) AND LOW COST.

2. Describe what you believe the biggest obstacles could be when implementing a token economy with your students. What could you do to overcome the obstacles?

3. Describe what you believe the biggest benefits could be when implementing a token economy with your students.

4. Think about a student you currently work with who you believe might benefit from a token-economy system. What steps would you need to take to implement this evidence-based practice based on what you learned from the chapter?

5. How will you determine what items—tangible or otherwise—would be rewarding for your students?

6. How will you determine how much each item will cost?

7. What type of token and token system would work best for your students?

8. Will you give the students the option of spending their tokens right away, or would you prefer they only spend them at a designated time? If the latter, how can you support your students in storing the tokens until they spend them?

9. After implementing the token-economy strategy in your classroom, answer this question: "What went well?"

10. Did you have any challenges implementing the token-economy strategy in your classroom? If so, what were they? What adjustments could make the token-economy strategy work better for you?

Chapter 4

Set Students Up for Success: A Guide to High-Probability Sequencing

Rosa is a tenth-grade student in general education at a suburban public high school. She enjoys going to school and being the chair of her high school's yearbook committee. Her passion is photography, and she hopes to make a career as a photographer after graduation. However, during algebra 1, she often refuses to comply and participates in various off-task behaviors (for example, looking up photographers on her phone during class time and refusing to complete assignments).

Ms. Maddox, Rosa's algebra 1 teacher, researches various research- and evidence-based practices to support Rosa in completing instructional requests. She observes Rosa's reluctance and low energy related to working on algebra 1 in the classroom. Ms. Maddox decides to implement high-probability sequencing with Rosa because she thinks it will help encourage Rosa in class. Consulting her school's behavior intervention-ist, Ms. Maddox learns how to quickly deliver a series of high-probability requests to Rosa followed by a low-probability request to increase Rosa's compliance. Ms. Maddox will verbally praise Rosa after each completed high- and low-probability request.

High-probability sequencing, as this scenario illustrates, involves making three to five high-probability requests of a student prior to asking the student to complete a low-probability request (Knowles, Meng, & Machalicek, 2015). *High-probability requests* are tasks the student is likely to do, and *low-probability requests* are tasks the student is unlikely to complete. High-probability sequencing increases the rate of reinforcement a student receives for compliance, in turn establishing momentum for continued compliant behavior (Wood, Kisinger, Brosh, Fisher, & Muharib, 2018). The idea is that momentum will continue when the student is asked to complete a less preferred or more challenging task. High-probability sequencing, which operates as a tier 2 intervention, is a well-researched, preventive, proactive strategy for students who demonstrate challenging behaviors, and it can be used in both general and special education and at the elementary and secondary levels. You may hear people use the term *behavior momentum* when referring to high-probability sequencing because the terms are often used interchangeably (Common et al., 2019).

Research shows high-probability sequencing to be an effective antecedent strategy for increasing compliance related to general requests, social requests, and transitions (Wood et al., 2018). Although high-probability sequencing is well suited for students who have challenging behaviors associated with noncompliance, it can be used to support a range of students, including students with and without disabilities (Common et al., 2019). K–12 teachers can use high-probability sequencing not only to improve student compliance but also to improve academic achievement, social-emotional learning, and communication.

This chapter clarifies each step of high-probability sequencing, moving through the data-collection process, identification of appropriate reinforcements, delivery of high-probability requests, additional data collection to assess the effectiveness of the strategy, and ways to honor students' cultural and linguistic diversity and incorporate their interests. The chapter wraps up with a Concluding Thoughts section and a reproducible page that includes reflective questions to ponder. The chapter will revisit the Rosa and Ms. Maddox scenario throughout to make the concepts of the chapter visible within an imaginary school context.

HOW TO IMPLEMENT HIGH-PROBABILITY SEQUENCING

First, identify problem tasks or requests that result in student noncompliance (low-probability requests) and simple tasks or requests the student will regularly complete or comply with (high-probability requests; Wood et al., 2018). It is important to collect data (for example, using an event recording or a scatterplot) to verify both problem and easy tasks (Landrum & Sweigart, 2014). You can adjust the list as necessary.

Once you have identified the list of requests, present the student with three to five high-probability requests followed by one low-probability request. High-probability requests need to be logical and have a clear connection to the low-probability request. For example, an independent mathematics assignment could consist of multiple single-digit addition problems followed by a double-digit addition problem. In the content area of reading and language arts, the teacher might ask the student to read several already-mastered sight words before asking the student to decode an unfamiliar word. Each occurrence should reinforce desired performance. Following are the steps to take to implement high-probability sequencing.

1. **Collect data to identify high- and low-probability requests:** Collecting data is important because it gives teachers a sense of where students may be struggling and what tasks particular students find easy or difficult to carry out. This step discusses the process of collecting data and developing a list of both high- and low-probability requests to implement.

2. **Identify specific reinforcements to use during high-probability sequencing:** This step explains how the primary reinforcement for completing a high-probability request is the verbal feedback embedded in the strategy. It also asserts that this verbal praise can be supplemented with tangible, extrinsic rewards such as those found in a token economy. It emphasizes the need for age- and development-appropriate reinforcements for students.

3. **Deliver high-probability requests with specific reinforcement after each request in rapid succession:** This step outlines the precise actions teachers take in delivering a high-probability request. It provides information on the pacing of these requests.

4. **Collect data to determine whether high-probability sequencing is an effective intervention:** Teachers must re-collect data on student compliance with high-probability requests in order to determine whether compliance has gone above the baseline. This step discusses re-collection and the implications of new data.

5. **Consider cultural and linguistic diversity:** This step views the importance of considering cultural and linguistic diversity through the lens of appropriate student responses to high-probability activities. It emphasizes awareness that appropriate responses may take a variety of forms.

6. **Incorporate student interests:** This step offers a reminder to learn students' interests before implementing a strategy; in this case, we

highlight the need to talk with students to get a sense of things they care about and the usefulness of student interest inventories.

Collect Data to Identify High- and Low-Probability Requests

Before teachers implement high-probability sequencing, it is important to collect data (Wood et al., 2018). These data are considered baseline data. Data collection can involve talking with the student, and even family members of the student, to determine which requests are low probability for that student. Teachers may then collect data to validate their sense of which requests and tasks students regularly do and don't carry out (Landrum & Sweigart, 2014). This validation can occur by directly observing students and using an event recording or scatterplot (chapter 2, page 35). Directly observing the student helps teachers know what the low-probability requests may be. For example, you may observe the student having difficulty following directions, or you may witness the student being noncompliant during independent tasks.

It is also important to know which requests are high probability for students. You may also determine this by talking with family members and the student and then validating it through direct observations (Wood et al., 2018). Once data are collected, a list of high-probability and low-probability requests is compiled (Landrum & Sweigart, 2014). Researchers typically consider 80 percent or higher compliance with a request to signify a high-probability request (Wood et al., 2018). Validate data following each high- and low-probability request to determine whether the assessment of what the student will and will not do is correct (Landrum & Sweigart, 2014). You can adjust the list of both high- and low-probability requests as necessary.

Identify Specific Reinforcements to Use During High-Probability Sequencing

Ms. Maddox modeled various important ways to effectively implement high-probability sequencing and reinforcements that coincide with this evidence-based practice. High-probability requests provide increased opportunities for positive feedback, which increases the likelihood of the student demonstrating the desired behavior. Positive reinforcement is expected to be embedded into high-probability sequencing (Knowles et al., 2015). For example, the teacher should deliver three to five high-probability requests to the student, each within five to ten seconds of the previous request's completion. In addition, the low-probability request needs to come five to ten seconds after the student completes the final high-probability request to continue the positive momentum.

Students should receive specific positive feedback immediately following compliance with each teacher request, thereby allowing for a positive student-teacher exchange, which is crucial to the success of the intervention (Landrum & Sweigart, 2014). For example, Ms. Maddox might say, "Thank you, Rosa, for taking out your pencil," after Rosa completes this first high-probability request. Verbal praise is a powerful social reinforcement; however, examples of extrinsic reinforcement include tangibles from the school or classroom token economy (chapter 3, page 55). As a reminder, educators inevitably want their students to work for intrinsic reinforcement when completing a task (Scheuermann & Hall, 2016). Educators must remember that student-specific reinforcement increases the likelihood of student compliance. Finally, it is important that the sequence of high-probability requests and the reinforcements are appropriate for the student's age and development level.

Deliver High-Probability Requests With Specific Reinforcement After Each Request in Rapid Succession

Once the teacher has identified three to five easy-to-follow high-probability requests, the low-probability request, and the reinforcers, it is time to try using this strategy. The entire process happens quickly. First, the teacher needs to get the student's attention by making eye contact and stating the student's name (Wood et al., 2018). Then, the first high-probability request is made. Immediately after the first request, typically five to ten seconds after completion, the teacher gives the reinforcer following compliance. This same sequence is repeated two or three more times, where a high-probability request is given and the reinforcement follows. Immediately following the last high-probability request and reinforcement, the teacher gives the low-probability request to the student. The student immediately receives the reinforcement for compliance with the low-probability request. High-probability requests need to be varied and gradually reduced over time.

High-probability sequencing is a quick and simple, evidence-based strategy to kick-start appropriate behavior (Scott, 2017). It encourages students to complete high-probability requests by receiving reinforcement, which most students with challenging behaviors may receive on a consistent basis. Using this strategy can help motivate students to try the more difficult low-probability request.

The following revisit of the Rosa and Ms. Maddox scenario illustrates how to implement high-probability requests with specific reinforcement.

On Monday morning, Ms. Maddox begins implementing high-probability sequencing with Rosa. After Ms. Maddox assigns the class five independent practice algebra 1 problems, she walks to Rosa's desk and asks her to take out her writing instruments for class. This is her first high-probability request. Rosa complies, and Ms. Maddox verbally reinforces Rosa's compliance by thanking her for getting her pencil. She then asks Rosa to put her name at the top of her worksheet (her second high-probability request). Rosa complies again, and Ms. Maddox verbally reinforces Rosa for completing the task and asks her to open her algebra textbook (her third high-probability request). Rosa complies, and Ms. Maddox verbally reinforces her by thanking her for being so responsible. Finally, Ms. Maddox asks Rosa to complete the first independent practice problem on the worksheet (the low-probability request). Ms. Maddox praises Rosa for beginning her algebra 1 assignment and tells her she is excited for Rosa to complete the task so she can earn a chosen reinforcement. Rosa finishes her assignment by completing the low-probability request and chooses ten minutes of free time to listen to music.

Now that you understand how to deliver high-probability requests with specific reinforcement after each request, and you've read a scenario of how to implement the strategy, you need to determine whether high-probability sequencing is an effective intervention for a student. In the next section, we will discuss data collection to determine the effectiveness of high-probability sequencing.

Collect Data to Determine Whether High-Probability Sequencing Is an Effective Intervention

Data collection is not over once you have determined what high-probability and low-probability requests are. You should also collect data when high-probability sequencing is being implemented to determine whether the strategy is effective for the student with challenging behaviors. When you are implementing high-probability sequences, data should show students complying with low-probability requests at a higher rate than baseline data state.

If high-probability sequencing is working, then the high-probability requests should be gradually reduced (Landrum & Sweigart, 2014). You can make adjustments in the high-probability requests and reinforcers based on data collected. However, if the strategy does not successfully prompt students to comply with low-probability requests after a few trials (three to five), you should stop using the strategy and try a different evidence-based strategy (Scott, 2017). Remember, there are times when a strategy is effective for some students but not others. Data collection serves as a driving force to help you understand why an evidence-based practice isn't working. If you have implemented the strategy with fidelity, and enough time has passed (which will vary depending on the strategy), then it's OK to try another evidence-based strategy. The point is to determine the strategy that works best for each student so that each can be successful.

Consider Cultural and Linguistic Diversity

It is important that teachers recognize their own knowledge of and attitude toward students from diverse backgrounds because those are powerful factors in student success (Obiakor, Bakken, Simpson, & Algozzine, 2010). Building relationships with students and their families allows teachers to tailor material for high-probability sequencing to meet students' diverse needs (Edwards & Edick, 2013). Moreover, understanding students' cultural background allows teachers to provide instructional processes that match their students' needs (Obiakor et al., 2010).

When developing and preparing your curricular materials, you are more likely to maintain students' attention and engagement if the content or subject is of interest to them (Kieran & Anderson, 2019). Select material for high-probability tasks based on the student's culture, and focus on the student's strengths (Fullam, 2017). Ask yourself, "What connections can I make to the student's background knowledge, perspective, strengths, and interests?" Use examples that are reflective of the students' lives and communities. Rather than celebrating diversity during a nationally designated month, a special week, or a specific time around a holiday, for example, continuously collect classroom materials and design assignments and activities that include multiple perspectives. It is best to deliberately include race and race history as a celebrated part of your classroom and curriculum.

A specific aspect of culture to keep in mind when planning for high-probability sequencing is cultural difference regarding communication. This is critical when you expect students to respond verbally. Because verbal communication norms vary across cultures, being cognizant of differences that exist can help ensure successful communication. Teachers working with students from diverse backgrounds must understand the many ways culture influences communication styles, preferences, and interpersonal interactions (Hwa-Froelich, 2015).

Understanding your students' communication preferences assists in establishing appropriate expectations regarding student responses to high-probability activities. For example, in many Western countries, independence is fostered, valued, and supported (Hwa-Froelich, 2015). In individualistic societies, people are motivated by their own needs and preferences, and personal goals are often prioritized over those of others (Yama & Zakaria, 2019). Students in these societies are taught and expected to think, talk, and act in ways that are independent of others. They are encouraged to be self-reliant and independent. A common example of this in U.S. schools involves IEP meetings for students with disabilities. Frequently, students' goals relate to achieving independence.

At the opposite end of the continuum, some societies value, foster, and support interdependence. In these societies, people often view themselves in terms of collective groups to which they belong, such as families or coworkers, and are motivated by the groups' needs and priorities (Yama & Zakaria, 2019). In interdependent societies, also referred to as *collectivist societies*, children are taught interpersonal responsibility; this means they learn to set aside their personal goals and preferences for those of the group (Hwa-Froelich, 2015). For activities such as high-probability sequencing, having students work in pairs in which they take turns responding can accommodate students who come from cultures that value interdependence.

Incorporate Student Interests

When considering students' interests, teachers must consider the cultural aspects highlighted in the previous section. They can ensure they are incorporating students' interests by learning what the students' likes and dislikes are. Teachers can learn this information by observing the students or asking family and friends (Wood et al., 2018). It is important to also talk to the students to learn about hobbies and interests they have outside of school.

An interest inventory is a great way for teachers to learn new things about their students. Teachers can easily incorporate an interest inventory (see figure 4.1) during a classroom lesson by having students rank activities on a scale of 1 to 5 or even use different types of faces as a scale. Many different examples of student interest inventories can be found online. Teachers can use interest inventories at the elementary *and* secondary levels. In lower elementary grades or in special education, where a student may not be able to read or write yet, a parent or teacher can help the student complete the inventory. Once teachers understand students' interests, they can use the information in lesson activities and materials students complete and in reinforcers students earn.

Name: Jase   **Birthday:** 3/28
My favorite color is: blue
My favorite hobby is: baseball
I learn best when: I am close to the teacher
I don't learn best when: I can't see the board

	I don't like it at all.	I don't like it very much.	I don't care either way.	I like it some.	I like it a lot.
How do you feel about school?	1	②	3	4	5
How do you feel about sports?	1	2	3	4	⑤
How do you feel about music?	1	2	③	4	5
How do you feel about art?	1	2	3	④	5
How do you feel about reading?	1	②	3	4	5
How do you feel about mathematics?	1	2	3	④	5
How do you feel about writing?	①	2	3	4	5
How do you feel about science?	1	2	3	④	5
How do you feel about social studies?	①	2	3	4	5

Figure 4.1: Example student interest inventory.

*Visit **go.SolutionTree.com/behavior** for a free reproducible version of this figure.*

EXAMPLES OF HOW TO UTILIZE HIGH-PROBABILITY SEQUENCING

Figure 4.2 (page 84) features three example subject-area task ideas. The sequence provided in example 1 begins with high-probability requests and then moves to the last prompt, which is the low-probability request. In example 2, we have two high-probability requests, followed by one low-probability request, and then we include three additional high-probability requests. Example 3 has the high-probability request at step 4. All the other prompts would be considered low-probability requests. Remember to include positive reinforcement immediately after each request.

Example 1: Writing Assignment

1. Take out your word web that we created yesterday in class.
2. Review the words and images you wrote and drew on it yesterday.
3. Circle the item on your web that you'd like to start with.
4. Write a sentence underneath that image that describes it.

Example 2: Addition Independent Practice Worksheet

One digit by one digit	$7 + 3 =$
One digit by one digit	$4 + 2 =$
Two digit by one digit	$10 + 2 =$
One digit by one digit	$3 + 5 =$
One digit by one digit	$2 + 7 =$
One digit by one digit	$6 + 4 =$

Example 3: Science Assignment

1. Write your name on your paper.
2. Look at the whole diagram.
3. Look at step 1 in the cycle.
4. What is the name of that step? Write your answer on the line underneath the image.
5. Check with your elbow partner. Did you have the same answer?

Figure 4.2: Three example tasks for high- and low-probability requests.

Now that you have an understanding of how high-probability sequencing is implemented based on the preceding sections, let's look at an example in the Rosa and Ms. Maddox scenario.

After six weeks of implementing high-probability sequencing with Rosa, Ms. Maddox reviews Rosa's completion rates for her independent algebra 1 classwork and her daily assignment grades. These data reveal substantial changes in the completion of her in-class algebra assignments. In addition, her daily algebra 1 grades show an increase of nearly 20 percent from the previous six weeks' grades. Ms. Maddox decides to continue implementing high-probability sequencing with Rosa for the next six-week period and then revisit the data. Once Rosa begins to consistently comply with low-probability requests, Ms. Maddox will start to fade the requests, that is, reduce the ratio of high-probability to low-probability requests. Ms. Maddox is optimistic about Rosa's success in her algebra 1 class.

The following text provides an alternate development in the scenario involving Rosa and Ms. Maddox. In this alternative, Rosa's grades have not increased as much after six weeks of implementing high-probability sequencing.

After six weeks of implementing high-probability sequencing with Rosa, Ms. Maddox reviews Rosa's completion rates for her independent algebra 1 classwork and her daily assignment grades. These data reveal only slight changes in the completion of her in-class algebra assignments. Her daily algebra 1 grades show only a 10 percent increase from the previous six weeks' grades. Ms. Maddox is unsatisfied with these results and decides to add a tangible reinforcement to coincide with this evidence-based practice and the verbal praise. Ms. Maddox and Rosa work together to identify what tangible reinforcement would help further motivate Rosa's progress in algebra 1. Ms. Maddox presents Rosa with a reinforcement inventory, and they discuss potential reinforcements together.

They decide that Rosa will be able to work on her yearbook committee photography assignments for the last five minutes of class after she has successfully completed her algebra 1 daily assignments. Ms. Maddox also decides to continue implementing high-probability sequencing with Rosa for the next six-week period and then revisit the data. Once Rosa begins to consistently comply with low-probability requests, Ms. Maddox will start to reduce the ratio of high-probability to low-probability requests. Ms. Maddox is optimistic about Rosa's success in her algebra 1 class.

We hope you feel confident in beginning to implement the evidence-based practice of high-probability sequencing. And we hope that you feel able to adjust that implementation as needed, as Ms. Maddox and Rosa did in this alternative scenario segment.

In table 4.1, we provide you with a short list of dos and don'ts for implementing high-probability sequencing in the classroom. When determining how to get started, refer to the dos and don'ts to help you as you implement high-probability sequencing in your classroom.

Table 4.1: Dos and Don'ts for High-Probability Sequencing

Do	Don't
✓ Quickly move through the sequence of high-probability and then low-probability requests.	✗ Allow for too much time lag between the high-probability and low-probability requests.
✓ Consistently use positive reinforcement after the student complies with each request.	✗ Shame the student for giving an incorrect response.
✓ Implement high-probability sequencing in general and special education classrooms.	✗ Attempt to implement high-probability sequencing during transition times of the school day (for example, in hallways while students are changing classes).
✓ Keep the intervention subtle.	✗ Delineate to the student which tasks or requests are high probability and which are low probability.
✓ Collect data to ensure the intervention positively impacts student performance.	✗ Preplan positive behavior supports to implement in instances when the student does not engage in an assigned task or directive.

CONCLUDING THOUGHTS

High-probability sequencing is a simple, quick, evidence-based tier 2 intervention to use in the classroom with students who display challenging behaviors (Landrum & Sweigart, 2014). It is important to create a plan based on data you collect before implementing the strategy. Once the plan is in place, the sequence of high-probability requests is immediately followed by reinforcement, which is then immediately followed by the low-probability request, and reinforcement happens very quickly. When thinking about high-probability sequences, ensure you are also considering your students' interests and any cultural or linguistic aspects that you need to ponder prior to implementing the strategy.

Next, we provide reflective questions to ask yourself as you are implementing high-probability sequencing. In the appendix (page 165), we have provided resources you can consult as you implement the high-probability sequencing strategy.

Chapter 4: Questions for Reflection

Write your responses to the following questions. Keep these responses in mind as you work to address challenging student behaviors and guide your students toward academic engagement and motivated learning.

1. Can you see yourself implementing high-probability sequencing within your classroom? Why or why not?

2. Describe what you believe the biggest obstacles could be when implementing high-probability sequencing with your students. What could you do to overcome the obstacles?

3. Describe what you believe the biggest benefits could be when implementing high-probability sequencing with your students.

4. Think about a student you currently work with who you believe might benefit from high-probability sequencing. What steps would you need to take to implement this evidence-based practice based on what you learned from the chapter?

5. What activities that you currently have in your class would be best suited to high-probability sequencing?

6. What activities would *not* be well suited to high-probability sequencing?

7. How does asking simple questions quickly for high-probability requests enhance the effectiveness of the strategy?

8. Think about a student you currently work with who you believe might benefit from high-probability sequencing. What steps would you need to take to implement this evidence-based practice based on what you learned from the chapter?

9. After implementing high-probability sequencing in your classroom, answer this question: "What went well?"

10. Did you have any challenges implementing high-probability sequencing in your classroom? If so, what were they? What adjustments could make high-probability sequencing work better for you?

Motivated to Learn © 2023 Solution Tree Press • SolutionTree.com
Visit **go.SolutionTree.com/behavior** to download this free reproducible.

Chapter 5

Teamwork Makes the Dream Work: A Guide to Classwide Peer Tutoring

Ms. Kennedy is a third-grade reading teacher at Central Elementary School, which is in a rural midwestern public school system. She typically teaches students in need of remedial reading instruction. Ms. Kennedy's classes include students with and without disabilities. Her students often read two to three years below their grade level and exhibit a lack of motivation to read. This year, Ms. Kennedy has observed that most of her students are having difficulty identifying the main idea in a text and are unable to distinguish between the main and supporting characters in stories. Ms. Kennedy determines she needs to learn more effective ways to teach reading and help motivate her students to read.

Ms. Kennedy attends a regional professional conference specifically related to educating students with academic difficulties. During one presentation, she learns about *classwide peer tutoring* (*CWPT*), an evidence-based, peer-assisted instructional strategy teachers can use to enhance students' reading accuracy. After attending this conference, she decides to implement CWPT within her classroom. Ms. Kennedy begins constructing activities and questions that will help her students practice their reading skills. She learns she needs to allot more time for her students to practice their reading in pairs so they receive immediate corrective feedback.

When Ms. Kennedy is ready to begin implementing CWPT in her classroom, she explains and demonstrates peer tutoring to her students. She gives her students time to practice tutoring in her class before she begins collecting actual data on this evidence-based practice. She models peer tutoring through role-playing with a fellow special education teacher to help her students better conceptualize this strategy. Through this role-playing, she provides feedback to her peer teacher and describes good tutor and tutee behaviors to her students. Ms. Kennedy teaches her students how to keep track of their partner's correct answers unassisted. Finally, Ms. Kennedy creates activities and games based on resources she already has, so her students will have fun with CWPT. She allows the tutors to reward their tutees with points for correct answers.

A variety of evidence-based, peer-assisted learning interventions is designed to help meet diverse students' academic and behavioral needs in inclusive, self-contained general and special education classrooms throughout preK–12 (Talbott, Trzaska, & Zurheide, 2017). The most widely recognized and researched peer-tutoring model is classwide peer tutoring, which strongly supports the use of peers to improve time on task, challenging behaviors, and academic achievement (Farley, Torres, Wailehua, & Cook, 2012). Additionally, peer tutoring such as CWPT has been shown to be effective for English learners, students at risk for academic failure, and students with attention deficit disorder, regardless of ability level (Hallahan et al., 2019). Academic achievement increases when teachers implement the CWPT model because it increases students' opportunities to receive one-to-one instruction, practice repeatedly, and receive immediate feedback (Farley et al., 2012). In the preceding scenario, Ms. Kennedy believes her students will greatly benefit from CWPT because they will get to work together and all students will actively engage in their learning when working together in this fashion.

The CWPT model involves reciprocal, mixed-ability pairs where students benefit from being both the learner and the teacher (Farley et al., 2012). Teachers can implement classwide peer tutoring across almost all content areas (mathematics, reading, social studies, and so on) using already-created instructional materials, which require minimal restructuring of teachers' lessons. The CWPT model was originally developed in the 1980s at the Juniper Gardens Children's Project, which established the following specific criteria (Maheady & Gard, 2010).

- Extra work is not created for the teacher.

- All students in the classroom benefit.

- Materials come from existing instructional resources.

- The model is intended to supplement rather than replace instruction.

- Tutoring takes place during existing instructional time periods.

Keeping the preceding criteria in mind, we delve into each step of the class-wide peer-tutoring strategy in this chapter. This chapter clarifies how to determine students' learning levels by administering a quick assessment prior to developing CWPT pairs and teams, and it outlines the building of pairs and teams and provides direction on choosing reinforcements. The chapter views cultural and linguistic diversity in consideration of the diverse ways students work in groups and the ways you can leverage student pairings to develop English language skills. It discusses how to model the tutoring process for students, and finally how to implement and monitor the activity. The chapter wraps up with a Concluding Thoughts section and a reproducible page that includes reflective questions to ponder. The chapter will revisit the Ms. Kennedy scenario throughout and at times compare that third-grade experience to that of an eighth-grade class. This scenario will make the concepts of the chapter visible within an imaginary school context.

HOW TO IMPLEMENT CLASSWIDE PEER TUTORING

Use classwide peer tutoring in place of independent work time after teacher-directed instruction. During CWPT, the teacher's role switches from primary instructor to a facilitator and monitor of the students' peer-teaching activities. According to curriculum and instruction experts Larry Maheady and Jaime Gard (2010), CWPT based on the original Juniper Gardens model has four components.

1. Weekly competing teams

2. Highly structured and reciprocal tutoring procedures

3. Points earned daily and at the end of the week, with the winning team earning a reward

4. Direct practice with purposeful instructional activities

The procedure for implementing CWPT is adaptable and based on the content area or grade (Farley et al., 2012). We have broken down the components of the Juniper Gardens model a little more to explain how teachers can effectively implement CWPT; that is, the Juniper Gardens model informs the following detailed steps. You will also find an example of the CWPT process for both an elementary classroom and a secondary classroom.

1. **Analyze assessment data:** This step leads teachers to discover where their students are developmentally with regard to the skill targeted for CWPT. It covers delivering quick assessments prior to building student pairs and teams.

2. **Pair students and develop teams:** This step gives teachers guidance on putting the pairs and teams together, emphasizing such considerations as the value of different learning-level pairings.

3. **Determine reinforcements with the class:** In this step, teachers learn about the importance of verbal feedback as well as the point system and other reinforcements.

4. **Consider cultural and linguistic diversity:** Considering cultural and linguistic diversity is always important. This step has teachers consider that important subject with regard to student behaviors in group activities, the building of empathy, and the development of language skills.

5. **Model the classwide peer-tutoring process for students:** This step covers explaining the activity to students, allowing students to practice it, and having conversations about what it means to be a good tutor and a good learner.

6. **Implement and monitor the peer-tutoring process:** This step outlines how to implement the activity, how to monitor its effectiveness, and how to keep students engaged with appropriate feedback.

Analyze Assessment Data

Before they can create classwide peer-tutoring pairs, teachers have students complete a preassessment or pre-activity. Typically, they use an assessment from the previous week to assign or adjust pairs (Farley et al., 2012). This assessment is used to determine the learning levels of students so that the teacher may create heterogeneous pairs, meaning pairs of students who are not on the same learning level. These assessments can be quite simple. In the chapter scenario, for example, Ms. Kennedy might have her third-grade students complete a quick assessment on answering simple narrative recall questions after a teacher read-aloud session. In middle or high school, the assessment might take a similar form. Let's say an eighth-grade teacher named Mr. Dykes uses the initial vocabulary quick check from the district-provided curriculum. Ms. Kennedy and Mr. Dykes examine the results of these assessments to see how to pair students.

Pair Students and Develop Teams

The teacher groups students into heterogeneous pairs based on assessment data. One student scored higher on the previous week's assessment, and the other student scored lower on the previous week's assessment, so the teacher ends up having a high-low pair of students.

In addition to pairing students based on assessment data, it is important to consider students' interests when creating pairs, and it is important to consider the dynamic that can occur between two students. You may find it helpful to look back at the student interest inventory (chapter 4, page 75). If students have not completed an interest inventory, have them do so. You can keep student interests in mind as you create pairs. Some students may not realize they have similar interests until they are paired for classwide peer tutoring.

The Juniper Gardens model divides pairs into two teams to compete for the highest number of points. New teams are formed weekly; this increases the probability that each student gets the opportunity to be on a winning team, and it also helps prevent cliques from developing (Maheady & Gard, 2010). For example, after Ms. Kennedy creates pairs based on assessment data and students' interests and cultural and linguistic needs, she works to evenly distribute the pairs into two teams based on the quick mathematics preassessment scores. Similarly, after creating pairs, Mr. Dykes evenly distributes the pairs into two teams—each with a similar number of high-low pairs—based on the quick vocabulary preassessment scores.

Determine Reinforcements With the Class

Typically, students with challenging behaviors do not receive consistent positive reinforcement. CWPT has built-in reinforcement because students receive peer and teacher reinforcement (Farley et al., 2012). The student tutor provides verbal reinforcement when the learner answers questions correctly, and the learner earns tally marks for correct responses. Additionally, the teacher walks around the room providing specific verbal praise and bonus points for appropriately participating in tutoring sessions. The winning team earns additional extrinsic rewards (for example, game or electronic device time). As previously stated, the teacher works to change teams to ensure all students earn the extrinsic rewards at the end of the week.

Teachers must make sure that reinforcement ideas match students' interests so the students want to work toward earning the reinforcement. Talking with the students about what interests them or reviewing the interest inventories they have already completed will help ensure reinforcements match students' interests. As a reminder, it is always important to verify students' interests because they can change; in addition, teachers can change tally marks to stickers, tokens, or tickets to meet students' needs. For example, Ms. Kennedy's class votes for extra recess time as their reinforcement. Mr. Dykes's class decides they will get free time at the end of class to listen to music or play a school-approved game on their electronic devices.

Consider Cultural and Linguistic Diversity

To make learning experiences more effective and relevant for ethnically diverse students, culturally responsive teachers use the cultural knowledge, prior experience, and performance styles of their students (Gay, 2018). More specifically, culturally responsive teachers have an understanding of their students' diverse backgrounds. For example, they know that Latinx families are often of collectivist cultures. Latinx students often are successful with cooperative classroom activities such as CWPT (Carney, 2021). Teachers need to create an environment that is accepting of cultural differences. Additionally, they should use instructional practices that are effective for all students, regardless of their background (Hallahan et al., 2019).

CWPT is designed to enhance the academic achievement and social skills of *all* students, and research has shown it to be an effective strategy for providing culturally responsive instruction to students from diverse backgrounds (Hallahan et al., 2019). Teachers are able to provide culturally sensitive instruction to students by pairing a peer who speaks limited English with a peer who is more proficient in English. This allows students to build language skills because peers typically have more language in common than teachers and students do, and they will converse more freely. Teachers who are culturally responsive focus on the strengths of their students and use cross-cultural communication skills and practices (Gay, 2018).

Model the Classwide Peer-Tutoring Process for Students

Up to this point, teachers have formed pairs and teams based on assessment data. They have considered students' interests and cultural and linguistic needs, and they have decided on reinforcements to earn. Now, it is time for teachers to model how classwide peer tutoring is done. Modeling for students how CWPT works is important. Follow these specific steps when modeling CWPT to ensure students understand what they will be doing.

1. Explain and model what the tutor and learner are supposed to do prior to beginning.

2. Explain to the class that they will get to be a tutor and a learner during the activity.

3. Explain what a tutor is and what a learner is. You may want to ask the class what they think a good tutor and a good learner look like.

4. Explain your role as the teacher. Tell the class you will be walking around the room looking for teams that are engaged in the peer-tutoring process.

5. Explain how students can get bonus points for working together as pairs and following directions.

6. Explain how teams earn points. Tell students that you created the teams and that the teams will change weekly. Show the class the tally sheets, and explain how the students earn points (two points for correct answers and one point for corrected answers).

Here, Ms. Kennedy models CWPT for her third-grade class.

Ms. Kennedy explains to the class that they will be doing a fun activity to help them advance their reading skills. She tells the students that she has paired them up and created two teams. (This is a good time to tell the students that they will find out their pairs and teams once directions are explained and understood.) She explains that they will each get to be a tutor and a learner; each person gets ten minutes to be a tutor and ten minutes to be a learner. (This is also a good time to show the students the timer.)

Ms. Kennedy talks about what a good tutor looks like. The tutor will show the learner a flash card with a reading vocabulary word on it and ask the learner what the word is. When the learner answers correctly, the tutor says things like, "Good job!" "You're right!" or "Great work!" She then explains what to do if the learner gets the answer wrong—for example, the tutor says something like, "That was a good try! The answer is *apple*. What is the word?" If the learner then gets it correct, the tutor gives positive feedback. "I'm scared to get a wrong answer," a student says. Ms. Kennedy says that whether the answer is wrong or right is not the most important part of the activity; rather, good learners must actively answer questions and, most importantly, simply try their best.

Ms. Kennedy takes a little bit of time and has volunteers practice being tutor and learner. She explains what to do as the students go, knowing that she must continue until she feels the students truly understand.

Ms. Kennedy decides to let the students pick the team names. They settle on the Bears and Lions—two strong and brave animals! Ms. Kennedy can tell that the students are already becoming engaged in the learning activity and gaining confidence. She can't wait to see how the excitement and budding confidence translate to better reading skills!

If Mr. Dykes models CWPT for his eighth-grade class, this modeling will likely look similar to the way in which Ms. Kennedy modeled the process for her third-grade class. Mr. Dykes could allot more time, such as fifteen minutes, for each role of tutor and learner, since his students are older and have more patience and longer attention spans. He also may choose to bring more open-ended discussions into modeling for his students. He might, for instance, ask them what a good tutor and a good learner look like, allowing them to weigh in through a broader discussion even as he clarifies his expectations.

Implement and Monitor the Peer-Tutoring Process

Pairs typically work together for twenty to thirty minutes three to five days per week. Each student takes the role of learner and the role of tutor for equal amounts of time. The teacher provides materials (for example, study guides and flash cards) for the tutor to use and sets a timer for ten to fifteen minutes. The tutor has the correct answers and provides positive feedback and acknowledgment and awards two points when the learner gives the correct answer. If the learner responds incorrectly to a question, the tutor stops the learner and models the correct answer. The tutor asks the question again to allow the learner the opportunity to answer correctly. The learner is awarded one point for the correction. After the timer goes off, the students switch roles and repeat the process for an equal amount of time.

While the students are working, the teacher walks around the room, randomly awards points to pairs for good tutoring, and consistently provides specific positive verbal reinforcement for their work. For example, if the teacher notices a pair maintaining a quick pace or hears a tutor using error-correction procedures appropriately, the pair can be awarded bonus points. The teacher can say, "Great work on maintaining that quick pace!" or "Jose, I like how you corrected Asher on that question. Good job using our error-correction procedures!" The teacher also provides assistance to pairs as needed. One thing to note: students at the secondary level may be more engaged if the teacher randomly awards points for appropriate interactions while circulating around the classroom rather than awarding points for each correct answer (Farley et al., 2012).

The following example illustrates how two students (Zoe and Artemus) might approach error correction during a whole-class tutoring activity to practice vocabulary words. Notice how the student acting as a tutor provides affirmations even while offering corrections and then asks the question again to give the learner the opportunity to answer the question correctly.

> Artemus holds a vocabulary flash card with the word *flexible* on it and says, "Zoe, what is this word?"
>
> Zoe replies, "Flexible."
>
> "You're right! Good work!" Artemus says. Holding up the next card, which features the word *furious*, he asks Zoe, "What is this word?"
>
> "*Frantic*," Zoe says.
>
> "Nice try," Artemus says. "The word is *furious*. What is the word?"
>
> "*Furious*," Zoe replies.
>
> "Good job! It is the word *furious*."
>
> This continues until the time is up, at which point it's Zoe's turn to be the tutor, and Artemus becomes the learner.

At the end of the session, pairs add up their points earned, including bonus points, and write their total under their team scoreboard that is posted in the classroom. Students are individually evaluated using existing assessment procedures based on what they practiced during the week's CWPT. Students can earn additional points for their team based on scores earned. For example, students can earn five points for themselves and their team for each mathematics problem they correctly complete on a test. At the end of the week, the winning team earns a certificate that each team member can sign (Maheady & Gard, 2010).

Here are step-by-step directions for implementing CWPT. These directions feature specific examples from the third-grade and eighth-grade classrooms of Ms. Kennedy and Mr. Dykes.

1. Teachers put the students in pairs and give each pair of students a tally sheet so they can tally the points they earn.

- Ms. Kennedy puts the class in pairs and gives each pair of students a phonics chart and vocabulary flash cards that have a word on the front and a corresponding image on the back for the tutor.

- Mr. Dykes puts the class in pairs and gives each pair of students flash cards that have a science term on the front and the definition on the back for the tutor.

2. Prior to beginning the tutoring session, teachers remind students how the points work. If a learner answers correctly, the learner earns two points. If a learner answers incorrectly, the tutor reminds the learner what the answer is and gives the learner another chance to correctly answer the question. If the learner then answers correctly, one point is earned.

- Ms. Kennedy asks for a volunteer to model what it looks like to be a tutor and learner when the learner's answer is correct, including the tutor's providing positive feedback and two points for correct answers. She asks for another pair to volunteer what it looks like to provide corrective feedback, including error correction and one point for the correction. Ms. Kennedy asks if there are any questions, and she answers those that come up.

- Mr. Dykes goes through the entire CWPT process by asking students questions about each step. They share their knowledge on each step. Mr. Dykes asks if there are any questions, and he answers those that come up.

3. After answering questions, teachers set their timers and tell the students to begin.

- Ms. Kennedy sets her timer for ten minutes and tells the students to begin.

- Mr. Dykes sets his timer for fifteen minutes and tells the students to begin.

4. As students begin, the teachers walk around their classrooms to monitor tutoring. When the teachers notice pairs correctly engaging in classwide peer tutoring, students earn an extra point and get specific verbal praise. The first time the students are doing CWPT, pairs receive bonus points and specific verbal praise each time their teachers see them correctly engaging in CWPT.

- As Ms. Kennedy walks around the room, she notices Ella and Colton working well together. She says, "Colton and Ella, I like how well you are working as a team! Great job! Give yourselves one bonus point." She notices Sara and Marisol and says, "Sara, I really like the words you used when you told Marisol she answered correctly. Give yourself a bonus point!" She notices Andrew and Michael and says, "Andrew, I like how you encouraged Michael when he answered incorrectly, told him the correct answer, and gave him the opportunity to answer again. Give yourself a bonus point!"

- As Mr. Dykes walks around the room, he notices Grace and Merus working well together. He says, "Grace, I like how you gave Merus positive feedback for answering the question correctly. Give yourself a bonus point!" Mr. Dykes notices that Sean and Mason stopped working as soon as the timer went off and waited for further instructions. He says, "Sean and Mason, thank you for stopping immediately when the timer went off. I like that you waited for me to see what to do next. Give yourselves a bonus point." Mr. Dykes hears Addison give appropriate corrective feedback. He says, "Addison, great work giving Jaylen the correct answer and another opportunity to answer. You gave great positive feedback when he answered the question correctly. Give yourself a bonus point!"

5. When time is up, teachers stop the pairs and announce it is time for pairs to switch roles. Teachers walk around their classrooms to monitor tutoring and help as needed while continuing to provide specific positive reinforcement.

   - At the end of the ten-minute period, Ms. Kennedy stops the group and states it is time for the pairs to switch roles. She reminds the group of the rules and asks the group if they have questions. She sets the timer for ten minutes and tells the pairs to begin.

   - At the end of the fifteen-minute period, Mr. Dykes stops the group, tells the pairs to switch roles, and answers questions students have.

6. When the timer goes off, pairs count their tally marks. All the pairs' totals are added to their respective team's scoreboard that is posted in the front of the room.

   - Ms. Kennedy gives the pairs time to tally their points. She gives them a minute to put their tally sheet in their reading data folder. She prompts one person from each pair to put their total number of points on the poster under their team's name.

▸ Mr. Dykes gives the pairs time to tally their points. He gives them a minute to put their tally sheet in their science data folder. He prompts one person from each pair to put their total number of points on the poster under their team's name.

Students engage in CWPT several times throughout the week. It may be beneficial to have multiple resources available for students to choose from when they engage in CWPT. For example, in reading, students may prefer an electronic copy of the text while other students may prefer a paper copy. Considering students' interests will help students be more engaged in their learning and can create new friendships, which ultimately helps create a more positive classroom environment.

Figure 5.1 includes tips for teachers to think about when preparing to implement CWPT and teach students how to be a peer tutor.

Elementary Level	Secondary Level
Decide in what content area you would like to implement CWPT. Pick an assignment or activity. For example, a language arts teacher might have students work on grade-level sight words. A mathematics teacher could use CWPT to teach multiplication facts.	Pick an assignment or activity to implement CWPT. For example, a Spanish teacher could have students work on a specific translation of various terms. A world history teacher might use CWPT for events and dates.
Create pairs based on assessment data.	Create pairs based on assessment data.
Gather materials tutors need to work with their learner.	Gather materials tutors need to work with their learner.
Explicitly explain and model how to be a tutor. Modeling will come from the teacher first. After the teacher models, a student can model, with the teacher providing reminders and assistance along the way. Modeling will occur until the students understand how to be a tutor. Students who are able to read (typically, students from the middle to the end of first grade and beyond) can have a checklist of the steps for how to be a tutor.	Explicitly explain and model how to be a tutor. Modeling will come from the teacher first. The teacher can pick a student to demonstrate the process to the class, with the teacher providing reminders as needed. The teacher can write down the steps of being a tutor for the students to follow.

Model the following steps, and create a checklist for tutors to follow. Gather materials, and find a spot to work in the classroom.

1. Wait for the teacher to start the timer and say, "Begin."

2. Show the flash card, and ask the learner the question on the card.

3. If the learner answers correctly, verbally reinforce the student. For example, say:

    a. "That's right!"

    b. "Great job!"

    c. "Nice work!"

4. Add two points to the tally sheet.

5. If the learner answers incorrectly, say the correct answer and ask the student the question again, saying, for example:

    a. "Not quite; the answer is _____."

    b. "The answer is _____."

    c. "You're close; the answer is _____."

6. When the learner answers correctly, verbally reinforce the student and add one point to the tally sheet.

7. Complete the preceding process of asking questions until the timer goes off.

8. After the teacher stops you, tally your points as a pair.

All students should receive an opportunity to practice being a tutor.

Model the following steps, and create a checklist for tutors to follow.

1. Gather materials, and find a spot to work in the classroom.

2. Wait for the teacher to start the timer and say, "Begin."

3. Show the flash card, and ask the learner the question on the card.

4. If the learner answers correctly, verbally reinforce the student. For example, say:

    a. "That's right!"

    b. "Great job!"

    c. "Nice work!"

5. Add two points to the tally sheet.

6. If the learner answers incorrectly, say the correct answer and ask the student the question again, saying, for example:

    a. "Not quite; the answer is _____."

    b. "The answer is _____."

    c. "You're close; the answer is _____."

7. When the learner answers correctly, verbally reinforce the student and add one point to the tally sheet.

8. Complete the preceding process of asking questions until the timer goes off.

9. After the teacher stops you, tally your points as a pair.

All students should receive an opportunity to practice being a tutor.

Figure 5.1: Tips for preparing to implement classwide peer tutoring at the elementary and secondary levels.

*Visit **go.SolutionTree.com/behavior** for a free reproducible version of this figure.*

EXAMPLES OF HOW TO UTILIZE CLASSWIDE PEER TUTORING

Teachers can adapt their use of classwide peer tutoring to target specific skills of content areas at both the elementary and secondary grade levels. For example, the following list shares a series of content-skill pairings.

- Spelling
  - Vowel-consonant-vowel
  - Vowel-consonant-vowel-silent *e*
  - Word families (for example, *-ash*, *-est*, and *-ight*)
  - Suffix adding
  - Consonant doubling
- Reading
  - Sight words
  - Fluency
  - Main idea
  - Prediction
- Vocabulary words
  - English language arts
  - Social studies
  - Science
  - Art
- Content facts for any subject
  - Location of states or countries
  - Mathematics facts (for example, addition and multiplication)
  - Algebra problem solving

Sometimes, trying a new strategy can feel overwhelming to already-busy teachers. The wonderful thing about CWPT is that teachers use current curriculum resources. They take questions directly from curricula but can simplify them to ensure information is accessible to all students (Farley et al., 2012). Teachers provide students with all materials, including the answer key. Figures 5.2 and 5.3 are examples of tally sheets that teachers can use.

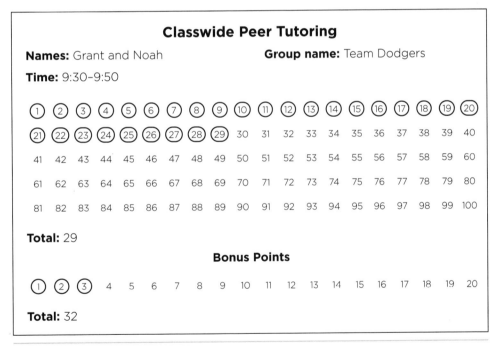

Figure 5.2: Tally sheet—Example 1.

*Visit **go.SolutionTree.com/behavior** for a free reproducible version of this figure.*

Figure 5.3: Tally sheet—Example 2.

*Visit **go.SolutionTree.com/behavior** for a free reproducible version of this figure.*

Now that we have gone through how to implement CWPT and shared examples of how to utilize CWPT in the classroom, let's look at the conclusion of the Ms. Kennedy scenario and how Ms. Kennedy implements CWPT in her classroom.

During the first six weeks of implementing CWPT, Ms. Kennedy observes numerous positive changes in her classroom. First, data collection from informal assessments shows that her third-grade students with reading difficulties are improving in their ability to read a passage and accurately identify the main idea. Additionally, most students are able to discern between the main characters and supporting characters of a story with 80 percent accuracy. These reading comprehension changes stem in part from greater reading fluency, which is a large share of what Ms. Kennedy has targeted with CWPT. Ms. Kennedy also observes better morale stemming from her students' opportunity for socialization that the CWPT practices allow. She observes her students being more encouraging of each other and more invested in their partners' success in the classroom.

Ms. Kennedy does have challenges with the implementation of CWPT. She observes two different pairs of students that struggle interpersonally while working on their daily reading activities. She discovers a common behavioral pattern among these four students who struggle with the evidence-based practice, specifically the two students with challenging behaviors. For these students, receiving immediate, corrective, and frequent feedback during their peer-group time causes defiant reactions. These students regularly argue, which often escalates to verbal aggression.

Ms. Kennedy works with her special education teacher to create scenarios that they can role-play specifically for these four students. Within these role-playing scenarios, the two teachers describe challenges such as accepting criticism, increasing prosocial skills, and reinforcing their partner. Ms. Kennedy also discusses the students' opportunity to each earn a chance to select a secret reward from the coveted treasure chest at the end of their CWPT sessions when they exhibit appropriate behaviors. Ms. Kennedy concludes that combining CWPT and reinforcement is a practical way to decrease her students' reading difficulties.

We hope you feel excited to implement classwide peer tutoring in your classroom. In table 5.1, we provide you with a short list of dos and don'ts for implementing classwide peer tutoring in the classroom. Remember these things as you think about planning for implementation with your students.

Table 5.1: Dos and Don'ts for Classwide Peer Tutoring

Do	Don't
✓ Make sure that materials are matched to the students' abilities.	✗ Use materials that the students will perceive as being too difficult; materials that are too hard will frustrate the students and may make them reluctant to participate.
✓ Base content on material previously taught through direct instruction.	
✓ Give all students opportunities to be tutors, even in subjects where they have problems; they will learn from tutoring other students, and they will gain more confidence in their abilities in those areas.	✗ Cover content based on new skills.
	✗ Allow only the students who are most proficient in the subject areas to be the tutors.
	✗ Assign pairs randomly.
✓ Take students' social and academic needs into consideration when assigning pairs.	✗ Assume students know what they are supposed to do in the group.
✓ Make sure students have a thorough understanding of the expectations.	✗ Allow students to assign their partner an official grade.
✓ Make sure there is a mechanism for accountability.	

CONCLUDING THOUGHTS

Classwide peer tutoring is a well-researched and widely recognized evidence-based practice to use not just with students who have challenging behaviors but with all students (Farley et al., 2012; Maheady & Gard, 2010). CWPT is considered a preventive tier 1 practice because it actively engages all the students in the classroom. When students are actively engaged in the learning process, they are less likely to engage in challenging behaviors.

Some benefits of CWPT are that the strategy is embedded with positive reinforcement, which is encouraging for students with challenging behaviors, and students learn from one another rather than always learning the content from the teacher. When implementing CWPT, be sure to pair students based on data; place them in pairs of a higher-performing student and a lower-performing student. Keep in mind students' interests as well as their cultural and linguistic needs. It is important that the teacher explain and model the process before beginning it to ensure students understand expectations. While students are working in pairs, the teacher is actively monitoring them by walking around the room. Students tally each correct answer.

After all tally marks are counted and totals are added for each team, the teacher provides the decided-on reinforcement to the winning team.

Next, we provide reflective questions to ask yourself as you are implementing classwide peer tutoring. In the appendix (page 165), we have provided resources you can consult as you implement the CWPT strategy.

Chapter 5: Questions for Reflection

Write your responses to the following questions. Keep these responses in mind as you work to address challenging student behaviors and guide your students toward academic engagement and motivated learning.

1. Can you see yourself implementing classwide peer tutoring within your classroom? Why or why not?

2. Describe what you believe the biggest obstacles could be when implementing classwide peer tutoring with your students. What could you do to overcome the obstacles?

3. Describe what you believe the biggest benefits could be when implementing classwide peer tutoring with your students.

4. Think about a student you currently work with who you believe might benefit from classwide peer tutoring. What steps would you need to take to implement this evidence-based practice based on what you learned from the chapter?

5. What can you do in your classroom to support classwide peer-tutoring initiatives?

6. What is an ideal schedule for the implementation of classwide peer tutoring in your classroom?

7. Describe a subject area and activity in which you'd like to try using the classwide peer-tutoring strategy.

8. After implementing classwide peer tutoring in your classroom, answer this question: "What went well?"

9. Did you have any challenges implementing classwide peer tutoring in your classroom? If so, what were they? What adjustments could make classwide peer tutoring work better for you?

10. For students who require a bit more support to successfully engage in classwide peer tutoring, what steps could you take in advance of the next session to make sure these students have the support they need?

Chapter 6

Put the Students in Charge: A Guide to Self-Monitoring

Eli, a third-grade student, has endured multiple challenges in his personal life that negatively affect his academic achievement and behavior at school. During his time in school, Eli's teachers have had reason to believe Eli is a victim of extreme neglect and emotional, physical, and sexual abuse. From kindergarten to the end of his second-grade year, Eli's challenging behaviors gradually worsened. Physical aggression directed at adults and destruction of class materials were common occurrences when Eli was asked to complete his classwork, especially his mathematics work. When he entered Ms. Benzi's special education classroom in third grade, he was a frail, bright, but out-of-control student. Ms. Benzi and a team of educational professionals work diligently to promote positive outcomes for Eli through motivational, behavioral, and academic strategies.

Testing shows Eli is cognitively advanced; however, he often lacks motivation to complete his academic work. Eli's mother and stepfather are apathetic about Eli's education and his progress. His parents rarely attend his IEP meetings and ask the IEP team to make all the decisions pertaining to Eli's education. His educational team's members know they are responsible for implementing evidence-based practices to promote Eli's success in the classroom. Eli's parents offer no assistance, nor do they try to promote his academic success within the home; this is not surprising, as they are Eli's abusers.

Eli is eligible for special education services as a student with emotional and behavioral disorders and specific learning disabilities in the area of mathematics. He receives special education services in a self-contained classroom. Ms. Benzi, the special education teacher for students with challenging behaviors, teaches Eli his core academic subjects (mathematics, English language arts, science, and social studies). Eli is included in general education settings for specials classes (music, art, and gym), lunch, and breaks.

Eli's IEP team determines he will access more time in general education classes as his out-of-control behaviors decrease. The team's members understand that based on the abuse at home, Eli will have days when his behaviors are inconsistent. They will have to be consistent with behavioral expectations for Eli, provide him with breaks throughout the day, and maintain constant communication with him. His IEP team designs an individualized behavioral management plan for Eli to help him sustain more appropriate behaviors in the classroom. The team also discusses various motivational strategies, such as self-monitoring and reinforcement, to incorporate in his educational environment to promote his educational success. Additionally, while they know they have limited control over what happens in Eli's life outside of school, the team members review and follow their district's protocols on reporting the child abuse they believe Eli is experiencing in his home.

Unfortunately, at some point in your career as an educator, you will likely encounter child abuse and neglect issues related to one of your students. When you are confronted with these situations, it is important to follow your school district's protocol for responding to this abuse, as Eli's IEP team does in the preceding scenario. Gather information on your school district's protocol for reporting child abuse and neglect. For example, Eli's classroom teacher, Ms. Benzi, is obligated to report each suspected incidence of abuse and neglect to the school nurse and building administrator and not expected or allowed, within the parameters of the district protocol, to report these incidences directly to the state child protective services department. In addition to following the school policies, we recommend documenting suspected incidences on a password-protected computer to maintain the student's privacy. Be sure to follow up frequently with your building supervisor, district representative, or caseworker to ensure these matters are being appropriately handled. You can text or call the Childhelp National Child Abuse Hotline at 1.800.4.A.CHILD or 1.800.422.4453. This hotline has professional crisis counselors available twenty-four hours a day, seven days a week, in over 170 languages. All calls are confidential. The hotline offers crisis intervention, information, and referrals to thousands of emergency, social service, and support resources. Finally, each U.S. state has contact information for reporting child abuse and neglect, which you can find on the Child Welfare Information Gateway website (www.childwelfare.gov/organizations).

Responsibly addressing suspected child abuse and reporting it to the correct people are very important, and so is managing your own mental health. Seeing a student you work with in a position of suffering can be frightening, painful, and traumatic, especially since the abuse happens outside your realm of influence and can make you feel powerless to help. Addressing your mental health at a moment like this might include meditation or a self-awareness practice like journaling. Educator and well-being advocate and coach Tina Boogren (2018) offers a selection of educator self-care tips and plans that may prove useful in her book *Take Time for You: Self-Care Action Plans for Educators*. Effectively managing your mental health when faced with a student who is experiencing abuse can also make you more available to that student. You are likely one of the student's only means to a safe environment. The strength of character and empathy with which you meet your student each day are important, as are the strategies you help your student develop in order to gain a measure of self-control, dignity, and a sense of ability to achieve academically in a sometimes dangerous and chaotic world. Self-monitoring is one such strategy.

Self-monitoring is a self-management strategy that you can use for students who exhibit challenging behaviors and experience challenging situations, even those as severe as what Eli experiences. Teachers can use the strategy across all grade levels and in both special and general education to improve social behaviors and academic achievement (Yell et al., 2013). Self-monitoring is considered a tier 2 intervention. It involves students' learning to keep track of their own behaviors using two specific components: (1) self-evaluation and (2) self-recording (Hallahan et al., 2019). Students learn how to evaluate their own behaviors and record whether the behaviors occurred. When students are consciously aware of their behaviors, they are better able to change the behaviors (McDougall, Morrison, & Awana, 2012). In the preceding scenario, Ms. Benzi decides Eli would be a good candidate for learning how to self-monitor because he is aware of his behaviors and can learn how to record the behaviors. Specifically, he knows that when he is angry, he destroys class materials. He has a sense of what motivates his behaviors.

Allison Bruhn, Sara McDaniel, and Christi Kreigh (2015) conducted a systematic review of the literature on self-monitoring interventions where they examined forty-one different studies. They wanted to better understand how self-monitoring has been used to improve outcomes for students with challenging behaviors. In reviewing the research, Bruhn and colleagues (2015) find self-monitoring improves off-task student behavior, classroom disruption, and negative social interactions. Additionally, they find that with self-monitoring, on-task behavior increases, as do work completion and positive social interactions. They determined that reinforcement is a critical component of self-monitoring and that contingent reinforcement helps improve behavior much more than noncontingent reinforcement does (Bruhn et al., 2015).

Contingent reinforcement means when students show appropriate behavior, they earn a reinforcement. On the other hand, *noncontingent reinforcement* means students receive reinforcement continually, and the reinforcement is not based on the student's appropriate behaviors. For example, in our opening scenario, Ms. Benzi and Eli decide on self-reinforcement after she teaches him how to monitor and evaluate his behavior. When Eli engages in appropriate behaviors, he can earn his preferred reinforcement (or contingent reinforcement). However, if he does not engage in appropriate behaviors, then he does not earn his preferred reinforcement.

This chapter begins by identifying the disruptive behaviors that are candidates to address with the self-monitoring strategy. It articulates how to set up both teacher and student systems for rating student behavior, guides teachers through using reinforcements, and shows teachers how to maintain sensitivity to cultural and linguistic differences by giving attention to student preferences. The chapter wraps up with a Concluding Thoughts section and a reproducible page that includes reflective questions to ponder. The chapter will revisit the Eli and Ms. Benzi scenario throughout to make the concepts of the chapter visible within an imaginary school context.

HOW TO IMPLEMENT SELF-MONITORING

To implement self-monitoring, utilize a check sheet with goals and a rating system. We will share examples of check sheets with goals later in the chapter. Teachers can change the check sheet based on students' unique needs and use it across all grade levels. Consider the setting in which the challenging behavior occurs and how often the behavior occurs. If the behavior occurs only a few times per day, you can develop a check sheet that the student reviews at the end of the school day. For example, perhaps a student requests to go to the restroom more frequently than is necessary. A check sheet reviewed at the end of the school day would be appropriate.

On the other hand, if the behavior occurs several times per class period, the self-monitoring check sheet will have a greater impact if the student reviews it in more frequent intervals, such as every thirty minutes or at the end of every class period. For example, a student who frequently leaves his, her, or their assigned area without permission or a student who regularly talks out of turn would benefit from reviewing the checklist in smaller intervals of time.

The specific steps for implementing self-monitoring are as follows.

1. **Determine the goals:** This step shows teachers how to identify students' behaviors that are challenging and which productive behaviors the student could display instead.

2. **Develop the rating system:** This step shows teachers how to create systems to monitor students' behavior, particularly focusing on age-appropriate self-rating.

3. **Teach scoring procedures:** Knowing how to evaluate their own behavior is critical to students' success with this strategy. This step shows teachers how to help students define appropriate and inappropriate behaviors through the use of discussion, critical thinking, and scoring.

4. **Review ideas for reinforcement:** This step makes clear that students need to take the lead in choosing reinforcements for this strategy, and it shows teachers how to do this.

5. **Consider cultural and linguistic diversity:** While self-monitoring is by nature culturally responsive because students are deeply involved in its planning and implementation, this step draws attention to the importance of respecting things like how a student would like his, her, or their name written on a scoring sheet, and so on.

6. **Incorporate student interests:** This step shows teachers how to create a reinforcement menu based on student interests and preferences.

Determine the Goals

Consider the behavior the student is displaying, and then determine what behavior you would like to see the student demonstrate instead of the challenging behavior. For example, if a student is taking an excessive amount of time to complete assigned work, you could utilize a timer to give the student a visual prompt to complete the work in a predetermined amount of time. After you have determined what behavior you want the student to demonstrate, engage the student in a conversation about his, her, or their behavior and why the new behavior is important. Make sure to use a supportive tone and avoid criticizing the student.

Before writing the goals, revisit classroom rules with the student, discuss the challenging behavior you have seen, and elicit the student's help in writing the goals for improving the behaviors. When writing the goals, use first-person language and make sure you state them in terms of what you *want* the student to do, not what you *don't want* the student to do. For example, the goal, "I won't leave my desk until I finish my work," could instead be written as, "I will stay seated at my desk until I've completed my work." Additional example goals include the following.

- "I will begin my independent work as soon as it is assigned to me."
- "I will finish all my work in class."
- "If I don't know how to do something, I will raise my hand and ask for help."
- "I will remain in my seat during independent work."

Develop the Rating System

The rating system gives your students a way to actively monitor their own behavior. Self-monitoring is similar to an individualized token-economy system. The difference between a token economy and self-monitoring is the teacher is monitoring behaviors in a token-economy system, but with self-monitoring, students are doing the monitoring. The rating system helps students keep track of their behavior.

The next step for implementing self-monitoring is to develop a rating system for the student to evaluate his, her, or their performance toward meeting the goals. Take into account the behaviors you want the student to work toward, determine the frequency with which the self-monitoring sheet will be reviewed, and develop a rating system that the student can easily follow. We will go into detail about the self-monitoring sheet later in the chapter. Again, use first-person language to encourage ownership from the student.

Here is a sample rating system for the upper-elementary and secondary levels. To use the following rating system, students need to understand the concept of the numbers and be able to read. Depending on the student, you could use this system for students in second grade through students in twelfth grade.

- 2 = "I did great!"
- 1 = "I did OK."
- 0 = "I did not make progress toward the goal."

For younger students and students who are unable to read (typically kindergartners and maybe some students in first grade), pictures can be more effective than numbers. The teacher can explain what each image equals.

- ☺ = "I did great!"
- ☺ = "I did OK."
- ☹ = "I did not do well."

The rating scale can be very simple, and offer even just two possibilities. A simple system is beneficial in that the student either did well or didn't do well. There is no wiggle room, and the system is cut-and-dried, which is also a drawback. This type of system may not be beneficial for students who are just beginning to monitor their behavior. And many students need to have the in-between, where they may not have done great, but they've made some progress. The preceding three-possibility system offers this in-between.

The scoring can also be much broader. For example, students could score themselves on a scale of 0–10, along a continuum of *no progress* to *excellent progress* toward the goal. Some students may benefit from a long continuum.

Teach Scoring Procedures

It is important that teachers teach students how to self-evaluate. When teaching a student how to self-monitor behavior, first talk with the student about the appropriate behavior (raising a hand to ask or answer a question, for example). The student needs to clearly define what the expected behavior is and how to do it (Scott, 2017). After discussing expected behaviors, model how to monitor behaviors, and practice with the student. When students are first learning to monitor their behavior, having the teacher monitor too is helpful. Students can also practice identifying their appropriate and inappropriate behaviors that are being monitored. The teacher and student then set a reachable goal for performance. Find a balance between too easy and too hard, and choose reinforcers for when students reach their goals.

You can set up scoring in one of two ways: (1) the student self-rates only (see figure 6.1, page 116), or (2) the teacher provides a rating in addition to the student's evaluation (see figure 6.2, page 116). In the first scenario, the teacher is still reviewing the student's rating to ensure the student is being honest. In the second scenario, when the student and teacher are completing the rating together, they both use the same sheet. The student will evaluate first, and the teacher will add a rating directly after the student finishes. They can have a quick discussion about how things are going during this time. The teacher and student compare their ratings and discuss any differences in them. It may be beneficial to have the student and teacher complete the self-monitoring sheet when students are first learning how to monitor their own behavior. As the student gets better at self-monitoring and rating appropriately, the student can move to self-rating only.

Goal	English Language Arts	Mathematics	Science
1. I will start my work as soon as it's given to me.	0 ①1 2	0 1 ②2	⓪0 1 2
2. I will finish my work in class.	0 1 ②2	0 ①1 2	0 ①1 2
3. If I don't understand how to do something, I will raise my hand and ask for help.	0 1 ②2	0 ①1 2	0 ①1 2

Figure 6.1: Student self-monitoring check sheet.

*Visit **go.SolutionTree.com/behavior** for a free reproducible version of this figure.*

Goal	English Language Arts	Mathematics	Science
1. I will start my work as soon as it's given to me.	**My Rating** 0 ①1 2	**My Rating** 0 1 ②2	**My Rating** ⓪0 1 2
	Teacher's Rating 0 ①1 2	**Teacher's Rating** 0 1 ②2	**Teacher's Rating** 0 ①1 2
2. I will finish my work in class.	**My Rating** 0 1 ②2	**My Rating** 0 ①1 2	**My Rating** 0 ①1 2
	Teacher's Rating 0 ①1 2	**Teacher's Rating** 0 ①1 2	**Teacher's Rating** 0 ①1 2
3. If I don't understand how to do something, I will raise my hand and ask for help.	**My Rating** 0 1 ②2	**My Rating** 0 ①1 2	**My Rating** 0 ①1 2
	Teacher's Rating 0 1 ②2	**Teacher's Rating** 0 ①1 2	**Teacher's Rating** 0 ①1 2

Figure 6.2: Teacher and student check sheet on the student's behavior.

*Visit **go.SolutionTree.com/behavior** for a free reproducible version of this figure.*

In figure 6.2, notice in science the student gave himself a zero for starting work as soon as he receives it, but the teacher gave him a one. Sometimes, students will be harder on themselves than their teachers are. On the other hand, the student thinks he finishes all his work in English language arts class, but the teacher rated him slightly lower. It is important that during times of disagreement, the student and teacher talk to determine a rating they both agree on. Maybe the student needs one prompt in science to begin working, so the student rates himself at a zero, but the teacher is proud of the student for needing only one prompt rather than four or five. In English language arts, the student may think all work is finished, but the teacher reminds him of a missing assignment. Differences in ratings will occur at times, and that is OK. Having teachable discussions where the student is learning and the student and teacher are working together is essential in truly changing student behaviors.

In figure 6.3, we provide an example of a self-monitoring form that Eli and his teacher, Ms. Benzi, from our scenario have filled out.

Name: Eli	Date: 10/20		
	1	**2**	**3**
1. **Have a positive attitude.** • Say positive comments to the teacher and your peers.	Student 2 ① 0 n/a	Student 2 ① 0 n/a	Student ② 1 0 n/a
• Do not grunt or growl when you receive a directive. • Avoid verbally aggressive behavior with others.	Teacher ② 1 0 n/a	Teacher 2 ① 0 n/a	Teacher 2 ① 0 n/a
2. **Be respectful.** • Listen. • Avoid blurting out.	Student ② 1 0 n/a	Student ② 1 0 n/a	Student ② 1 0 n/a
• Follow directions. • Keep your eyes on the speaker.	Teacher ② 1 0 n/a	Teacher ② 1 0 n/a	Teacher 2 ① 0 n/a

Figure 6.3: Eli's self-monitoring check sheet.

continued →

3. **Demonstrate self-control.** • Keep your hands and feet to yourself. • Use materials appropriately.	**Student** 2 ① 0 n/a	**Student** 2 ① 0 n/a	**Student** ② 1 0 n/a
	Teacher 2 ① 0 n/a	**Teacher** 2 ① 0 n/a	**Teacher** 2 ① 0 n/a
4. **Do your best.** • Stay on task. • Persist with the task even when you are frustrated. • Ignore your peers and focus on yourself.	**Student** ② 1 0 n/a	**Student** ② 1 0 n/a	**Student** ② 1 0 n/a
	Teacher 2 ① 0 n/a	**Teacher** 2 ① 0 n/a	**Teacher** ② 1 0 n/a

[Insert an image of something that the student likes and will find relatable. Examples include popular live-action or animated movies, animals or foods, children's television characters, superheroes, and even anime.]

In the preceding figure, the numbers in the columns represent the following: 2 = *you did great*, 1 = *you did average*, 0 = *this needs improvement*, and n/a = *not observed*. The numbers at the top of the self-monitoring sheet represent the three intervals when Ms. Benzi observed the behaviors.

Review Ideas for Reinforcement

Teachers should create opportunities for students to earn reinforcements with the self-monitoring strategy. Research supports the effectiveness of pairing self-monitoring with reinforcement (Bruhn et al., 2015). Specifically, researchers Tonya N. Davis and colleagues (2014) analyzed the effects of self-monitoring with and without reinforcements in the classroom, and their findings reveal only self-monitoring and reinforcement combined significantly influence on-task behaviors in the classroom. While previous studies have shown self-monitoring in isolation is sufficient to enhance on-task behaviors in students, the pairing of the two helps students move toward positive behavior change. Researchers in the field of education have found that coupling self-monitoring and reinforcement enhances the students' motivation in the classroom (Bruhn et al., 2015; Davis et al., 2014).

The power of the self-monitoring strategy increases when the students can choose their reinforcement. The teacher may want to administer a reinforcement menu to help delineate what rewards work best for this strategy. The trick, like with the other evidence-based practices we've talked about in this book, is to ensure the reinforcers are things the students like and want to earn. From reading the preceding chapters, you know the importance and value of positive reinforcement and the impact it has on changing problem behaviors.

The reinforcements can be set up in multiple ways.

- The student gets reinforcement for any attempt to use the self-monitoring checklist.

- The student gets reinforcement for meeting some predetermined goal—all 2s or all 1s, for instance (see figure 6.1, page 116).

- The teacher and student rate the student's behavior. If the student and teacher both rate or agree that the student exhibits on-task behavior at least 80 percent of the time, for example, then the student earns a reinforcement.

Consider Cultural and Linguistic Diversity

Self-monitoring is inherently culturally responsive because the student is involved in all aspects of developing and implementing the intervention. As we mentioned earlier, teachers should involve students in developing the goals. Involving the students in goal development provides them with ownership of the strategy and may also give the teacher insights into how the students perceive their own abilities.

Strengths, preferences, culture, preferred language, and other characteristics unique to the student should be at the forefront of the design of the self-monitoring checklist. If a student's native language is a language other than English, ask the student which language he, she, or they would prefer be used on the form. Many websites can quickly and easily do the translating for you, including Google Translate (https://translate.google.com) and Free Translation Online (https://translation2.paralink.com). Middle and high school students may not want any designs or graphics on their forms, while elementary school students might find having images of their favorite characters on their check sheet to be very reinforcing. Of course, these examples are broad generalizations. The key is to communicate with students to gain information about their preferences when you are creating the form.

Some students might prefer that the form be used very discreetly. Remember, the purpose of this intervention is to support students, not to give them some type of punishment. If you have a student who does not want peers to be aware of the form, brainstorm with the student how you can keep all aspects of implementation low-key. Such ideas might include the following.

- When introducing the form, discuss it with the student in private, or at the very least, try to make sure the other students cannot overhear the conversation.

- Make the checklist on plain white paper with minimal detail (unless the student requests otherwise).

- The student can keep the checklist out of sight in a desk, binder, or backpack until the end of the class period, when it is time for the student to self-evaluate.

- At the end of the class period, when it is time to review the self-monitoring sheet, you can nonverbally signal the student to meet in a predetermined spot to review the form.

- Instead of having the student bring the checklist to you at the end of the class period, you can go to the student and quietly review it.

Incorporate Student Interests

When you are deciding on reinforcers to link to the self-monitoring checklist, you must consider students' interests and preferences. Students will not work to earn a reinforcer that does not hold value to them! Just the same, a highly valued reinforcer will motivate a student to work for it. An example of a reinforcement checklist appears in figure 6.4. The teacher is able to create a reinforcement menu based on the student interest checklist or survey the student completes.

Part 1: Sentence Completion

Directions: Complete the following statements.

1. My favorite adult at school is: Mrs. Boyd

   The things I like to do with this adult are:
   talk about the things I think and read books

2. My best friend at school is: Andrew

   Some things I like to do with my best friend at school are:
   lift weights and draw

3. Some other friends I have at school are: Mason, Tucker, Fischer, and Everett

   Some things I like to do with them are: play sports and hang out

4. When I do well in school, a person I'd like to know about it is: my mom

5. When I do well in school, I wish my teacher would:
   tell me I did a good job

6. **At school, I'd like to spend more time on:** doing fun things in school and not just sitting listening to the teachers talk all the time

7. **One thing I'd really like to do more in school is:**
    do fun projects with my friends

8. **When I have free time at school, I like to:** draw

9. **I feel great in school when:** I feel successful

10. **The person who likes me best at school is:**
    I don't know. Probably Andrew.

    I think this person likes me because:
    we've known each other a long time

11. **I will do almost anything to keep from:**
    having a lot of homework

12. **The kind of punishment at school that I hate most is:**
    I don't know

13. **I sure get mad at school when I can't:**
    get all my work done. I don't like having homework.

14. **The thing that upsets my teachers the most is:**
    when they yell at me in my face and blame me for things I didn't do

15. **The thing that upsets me the most is:**
    when I get yelled at in front of everyone

Part 2: Reinforcers

Directions: Check all that apply.

Favorite Edible Reinforcers

☑ Candy (specify): <u>Hot Tamales</u>

☑ Fruit (specify): <u>Apples and oranges</u>

☑ Drinks (specify): <u>Gatorade</u>

☑ Cereal (specify): <u>Peanut butter and chocolate Cheerios</u>

☑ Snacks (specify):
  <u>KIND bars, fruit, Smoothie King</u>

☐ Nuts (specify): <u>I don't like nuts.</u>

☑ Vegetables (specify): <u>Carrots</u>

☐ Other (specify): _____

Academic Reinforcers

☐ Going to the library

☑ Having good work displayed

☑ Getting good grades

☑ Having my parents praise good schoolwork

☐ Giving reports

☑ Making projects

☐ Completing creative-writing projects

Figure 6.4: Opportunities-to-respond action plan.   *continued →*

☑ Earning teacher praise

☐ Helping grade papers

☑ Getting a good note home

☐ Earning stickers, points, and so on

☐ Other (specify): _____

Favorite Tangible Items

☐ Stuffed animals

☑ Pencils, markers, or crayons

☐ Paper

☐ Trucks or tractors

☑ Sports equipment

☐ Toys

☐ Books

☐ Puzzles

Activity Reinforcers

☑ Coloring, drawing, and painting

☐ Making things

☐ Going on field trips

☐ Taking care of and playing with animals

☑ Going shopping

☑ Eating out in a restaurant

☐ Going to the movies

☐ Spending time alone

☐ Reading

☑ Having free time in class

☑ Having extra gym or recess time

☐ Working on the computer

☐ Other (specify): _____

Social Reinforcers

☐ Teaching things to other people

☐ Being the teacher's helper

☑ Spending time with my friends

☑ Spending time with the teacher

☐ Spending time with the principal

☐ Spending time with _____

☐ Having class parties

☑ Working with my friends in class

☐ Helping keep the room clean

☑ Being a tutor

☑ Being a leader in class

☐ Other (specify): _____

Recreation and Leisure Reinforcers

☑ Listening to music

☐ Singing

☐ Playing a musical instrument

☑ Watching TV

☐ Cooking

☐ Building models

☐ Doing woodworking and carpentry

☑ Playing sports (specify): <u>Cross-country, football, basketball, track</u>

☐ Working with crafts

☐ Other (specify): _____

☐ Other (specify): _____

*Visit **go.SolutionTree.com/behavior** for a free reproducible version of this figure.*

A student reinforcement survey takes the guesswork out of figuring out what is reinforcing to your students. We want to introduce you to Adrian, a middle school student who has challenging behaviors of a very different form than Eli's with very different contributing factors.

Adrian is a seventh-grade student on the autism spectrum. He loves ninjas. Often during direct instruction or independent work, he will stand up next to his desk and move through a series of ninja poses and strikes. Ms. Warren works with Adrian to review the class rule about remaining seated while she is teaching the class and while students are doing independent work. Adrian acknowledges that this is something he can work on.

Knowing that Adrian's native language is Spanish, Ms. Warren asks Adrian whether he would like the check sheet to be written in Spanish or English. Adrian says he would like the goals to be written in Spanish and then says something Ms. Warren is not expecting. He knows the Japanese symbols for the numbers 1–10, and he asks Ms. Warren if the rating system can use those. A quick internet search shows that the Japanese characters are readily available and will be simple for Ms. Warren to include on the check sheet! Adrian is highly motivated to use a checklist that connects to both his linguistic background (Spanish) and one of his interests (Japanese). The reinforcer Adrian will work toward for remaining seated is that he will earn time to get out of his seat and move through the ninja poses and strikes.

This example of implementing self-monitoring with a student who is very different from Eli shows how easily teachers can tailor self-monitoring to meet individual student needs. Now let's return to our original scenario with Eli.

Upon entering the special education classroom, Ms. Benzi quickly discovers that Eli's disposition toward his educational team and his mathematics assignments has changed for the better now that he has more accountability through self-monitoring. In addition to the self-monitoring checklist, the team implemented immediate reinforcement that coincides with his self-monitoring goals. When he earns a smiley face, he receives verbal praise. When he earns five smiley faces, he earns five minutes of free reading time at the end of the class period. Eli picks his reinforcements and often picks independent reading time. Eventually, the educational team is able to fade these self-monitoring procedures.

At the beginning of his individualized behavioral management plan, self-monitoring strategy, and reinforcement implementation, Eli was disappointed his family did not show the same positivity. Then he quickly expressed his approval for this type of reinforcement at school.

Three years later, Eli transitions to the general education classroom for the entire school day with little support from his special education team. Eli's stepfather has left the family, so the physical abuse has ceased; however, his teachers suspect that Eli's mother and other family members continue to neglect him. Despite Eli's current home climate, he maintains appropriate behavior and good grades at school. He writes his special education team a gratitude letter. "My old teachers are my only family," he says. "I wish they knew how much they changed my life."

EXAMPLES OF HOW TO UTILIZE SELF-MONITORING

When thinking about how self-monitoring can be used, it is important to remember that this strategy works best when students are aware of their behaviors and can record the behaviors. Self-monitoring is based on the specific behaviors that need to be changed for an individual student and will look different for each student. The following are examples of behaviors that can be expressed in a disruptive, off-task way, and which may be good candidates for the self-monitoring strategy.

- Requesting a drink of water
- Requesting to use the restroom
- Requesting to sharpen a pencil or get a different writing utensil
- Arguing with the teacher or another student
- Tapping writing utensils on the desk
- Talking to peers without permission
- Leaving designated areas without permission
- Making bodily noises
- Not following directions
- Not controlling the physical body
- Taking an excessive amount of time to engage in an assignment
- Not completing an assignment in the allotted time
- Failing to complete and return homework
- Showing off-task behavior during group or independent work

Self-monitoring is a versatile and effective evidence-based practice. As you think about implementing this tier 2 strategy with a student, keep in mind the dos and don'ts of implementing self-monitoring. In table 6.1 (page 126), we provide you with a short list of dos and don'ts for implementing self-monitoring checklists in the classroom.

CONCLUDING THOUGHTS

Self-monitoring is a tier 2 evidence-based practice to support students in monitoring and evaluating their own behavior. Self-monitoring decreases students' challenging behaviors, and rather than the teacher always monitoring them, students learn to do it themselves. If you are thinking about implementing self-monitoring with a student, remember that it is most beneficial in helping students maintain behaviors they have already learned. It is not an appropriate strategy for teaching new target behaviors (Scott, 2017).

Table 6.1: Dos and Don'ts for Self-Monitoring Checklists

Do	Don't
✓ Let the student know you are very excited about this new tool that will help the student. ✓ Use the checklist consistently. ✓ Involve the student in the development of the checklist. ✓ Help the student keep up with the sheet throughout the day. ✓ Remind the student of the reinforcement being earned that is associated with this self-monitoring strategy. ✓ Make sure reinforcement is based on student interests.	✗ Introduce the self-monitoring check sheet as a punishment. ✗ Use the checklist inconsistently. ✗ Develop the checklist on your own and then present it to the student. ✗ Punish the student if the student accidentally misplaces the sheet or forgets to provide a self-rating. ✗ Forget to reinforce the student when the student meets the self-monitoring strategy or goal. ✗ Create a list of reinforcements without considering student interests.

When implementing self-monitoring with a student, be sure to first teach the student how to self-monitor one's behaviors. For your students to be successful, you need to set them up for success. Teaching, modeling, and practicing are critical steps you can't skip. Thinking about appropriate reinforcers for the student to earn is also important. If you haven't had your students complete an interest inventory for reinforcements, this is a great opportunity to do that. Don't forget your students are learning and will make mistakes. Working through the mistakes will help your students succeed at not only monitoring their behaviors but also changing those challenging behaviors into more appropriate behaviors.

Next, we provide reflective questions to ask yourself as you are implementing self-monitoring. In the appendix (page 165), we have provided resources you can consult as you implement the self-monitoring strategy.

Chapter 6: Questions for Reflection

Write your responses to the following questions. Keep these responses in mind as you work to address challenging student behaviors and guide your students toward academic engagement and motivated learning.

1. Can you see yourself implementing self-monitoring within your classroom? Why or why not?

2. Describe what you believe the biggest obstacles could be when implementing self-monitoring with your students. What could you do to overcome the obstacles?

3. Describe what you believe the biggest benefits could be when implementing self-monitoring with your students.

4. Think about a student you currently work with who you believe might benefit from self-monitoring. What steps would you need to take to implement this evidence-based practice based on what you learned from the chapter?

page 1 of 2

5. How would you communicate to a parent or guardian that you are going to begin this intervention with a student? What would you say to communicate that the intervention is meant not to punish but to support the student?

6. For what behaviors would self-monitoring be appropriate for a teacher to use?

7. For what behaviors would self-monitoring be inappropriate for a teacher to use?

8. Describe some examples of when you would provide students with reinforcement for successful self-monitoring.

9. When do you think it would be most appropriate for a student to no longer use self-monitoring? What steps would you take to fade reinforcements?

10. After implementing self-monitoring in your classroom, consider this: Did you have any challenges? If so, what were they? What adjustments could make self-monitoring work better for you?

Chapter 7

Call on Students: A Guide to Opportunities to Respond

Ms. Lumpkins, a seventh-grade teacher, is struggling to keep her students focused and motivated to learn. Some students are exhibiting challenging behaviors, such as being inattentive when Ms. Lumpkins is talking, not following directions, and socializing with peers during independent work time. She feels like the students' challenging behaviors are taking away from her instructional time. Typically, she will do a whole-group lesson and ask students questions about the material they are learning. They will then independently complete a class assignment about the material.

Ms. Lumpkins talks to her mentor teacher, Mrs. Rueter, about the challenges she is having with some of her students. Mrs. Rueter tells her about the strategy of implementing a higher rate of opportunities to respond. Ms. Lumpkins thinks this sounds like an interesting idea when Mrs. Rueter tells her this strategy not only increases academic achievement but also decreases challenging behaviors. She thinks she will try it. Mrs. Rueter explains that before Ms. Lumpkins starts implementing a higher rate of opportunities to respond, she will observe Ms. Lumpkins teach a lesson to get an idea of what her current rate of opportunities to respond is. They set up a time the following week for Mrs. Rueter to observe Ms. Lumpkins.

After Mrs. Rueter observes Ms. Lumpkins teaching to see how many opportunities to respond she provides her students, Ms. Lumpkins works with Mrs. Rueter to create a plan for implementing more opportunities to respond in her classroom. Ms. Lumpkins is excited to increase her rate of opportunities to respond so she can help her students be successful in her classroom.

An important component of successful classroom management is effective instruction. This instruction includes utilizing strategies to maximize the possibility that students participate, actively respond, and also respond correctly (Haydon, MacSuga-Gage, Simonsen, & Hawkins, 2012).

As the opening scenario illustrates, receiving a high rate of opportunities to respond is effective across all ages in both general and special education. Opportunities to respond (OTRs) have been found to improve both behavioral and academic outcomes across a diverse population of students. Specifically, using OTRs increases on-task behaviors, academic engagement, and desired social behaviors while also decreasing disruptive behaviors and undesired social behaviors (Van Camp, Wehby, Martin, Wright, & Sutherland, 2020). Research also shows higher rates of OTRs increase students' academic performance (Haydon et al., 2012). Students' academic achievement increases because OTRs promote and support active student engagement and participation in class. Additionally, increasing rates of OTRs allows teachers more opportunities to give praise to students, which is also shown to foster positive student outcomes (Van Camp et al., 2020).

When implementing OTRs, the teacher asks a question (for example, "What is the capital of Ohio?"), the students respond (all students respond in unison, "Columbus!"), and the teacher provides feedback ("You're right! The capital of Ohio is Columbus!"). OTRs can be delivered by the teacher, peers, or technology. Plickers, Kahoot!, and Socrative are examples of technology to use when implementing OTRs (Rila, Estrapala, & Bruhn, 2019). Ashley Rila, Sara Estrapala, and Allison Leigh Bruhn (2019) go into great detail on each option in their article "Using Technology to Increase Opportunities to Respond." In the previous scenario, Ms. Lumpkins might ask students to give a thumbs-up or thumbs-down when they review a topic taught in class the day before, giving her an opportunity to quickly see who understands the topic and who may need more help.

This chapter provides step-by-step instructions on how to implement opportunities to respond, noting the granular aspects of determining the current rate of OTRs, developing a plan to increase them, and putting that plan in place. It also highlights the importance of considering cultural and linguistic diversity when implementing this strategy and of considering students' unique interests and using those interests to inform reinforcement ideas. The chapter wraps up with a Concluding Thoughts section and a reproducible page that includes reflective questions to ponder. The chapter will revisit the Ms. Lumpkins scenario throughout to make the concepts of the chapter visible within an imaginary school context.

HOW TO IMPLEMENT OPPORTUNITIES TO RESPOND

Typically, teachers rely on individual responses as their main way of giving students opportunities to respond to questions they ask. For example, a teacher may ask the class to solve an algebra problem in their notes and call on one student to provide the answer. When providing OTRs, the teacher may need to give instructional prompting while also allowing for response wait time and corrective feedback; for example, the teacher may engage in error correction and progress monitoring (Haydon et al., 2012). However, individual responses do not allow all students to experience high rates of OTRs during teacher-directed lessons.

Prior to adopting a higher rate of OTRs, teachers need to plan, implement, and monitor their use of OTRs. Guidelines set forth by the Council for Exceptional Children (1987) say students should have the opportunity to respond four to six times per minute with 80 percent accuracy during teacher-directed lessons. However, research supports positive student outcomes with rates of three to five OTRs per minute during teacher-directed lessons (MacSuga-Gage & Simonsen, 2015). Optimal OTR rates will depend on the type of instruction, the content, and the type of response required. Rila and colleagues (2019) suggest different rates of opportunities to respond based on the type of content students are learning.

- When students are practicing and doing drills (such as on mathematics facts) or when students are reviewing content, they should have eight to twelve opportunities to respond per minute.

- When teaching new content, teachers should deliver opportunities to respond four to six times per minute.

- When students are providing simple responses, teachers should deliver opportunities to respond three to five times per minute.

- Content requiring more complex responses will involve one opportunity to respond per minute.

The following are the steps for implementing opportunities to respond.

1. **Determine the current rate of opportunities to respond:** This step involves self-awareness, asking teachers to monitor how often they already provide students with opportunities to respond to simple questions in class. It emphasizes the need to collect data to make this determination.

2. **Develop a plan to increase opportunities to respond:** In this step, teachers use baseline data to create a plan to increase opportunities to respond.

3. **Implement the action plan:** Certain lessons lend themselves more easily to opportunities to respond. In this step, teachers consider which ones and then try out those lessons, taking care to allow students adequate response time.

4. **Monitor and adjust the plan as necessary:** Use this step to employ self-awareness once again to collect data on the effectiveness of the strategy. Get monitoring help from a colleague if necessary.

5. **Review ideas for reinforcement:** This step guides teachers in choosing reinforcements for the strategies, noting the importance of consistent verbal reinforcement.

6. **Consider cultural and linguistic diversity:** Since opportunities to respond involve so much verbal exchange, it is particularly important to know and pronounce all students' names correctly. This step makes this clear as well as emphasizing the need to engage students from all cultural and linguistic backgrounds.

7. **Incorporate student interests:** This step guides teachers in providing students with autonomy by learning and incorporating their interests into the strategy.

Determine the Current Rate of Opportunities to Respond

Teachers can determine the current rate of OTRs in their classroom through monitoring themselves (that is, collecting data on their own performance) or asking a colleague or administrator to monitor their use of OTRs. Data collection should occur over three to five days for short time periods (for example, ten to fifteen minutes).

To get an average number of OTRs at the end of the observation period, the teacher divides the number of OTRs by the number of minutes observed. If a teacher named Mr. Favre has six opportunities to respond in a fifteen-minute period, the rate would be 0.4 OTRs per minute. If the teacher presents a total of eight opportunities to respond in that time, then the rate would be 0.53 (8 divided by 15). The rate is graphed on the daily data sheet.

Develop a Plan to Increase Opportunities to Respond

Typically, teachers' number of opportunities to respond is low (sometimes an average of less than one opportunity to respond per minute). Before a teacher can implement a plan to increase that number, it is important that the teacher get baseline data, as outlined in the preceding section, to determine how many OTRs are delivered in a specific time period (for example, fifteen minutes). The goal for increasing OTRs should be based on the content being taught (Rila et al., 2019). For example, content may be practicing math facts. Reviewing and practicing math facts will be delivered at the highest rates of eight to twelve per minute because students can respond quickly to this kind of fact-based recall. Todd Haydon, Ashley S. MacSuga-Gage, Brandi Simonsen, and Renee Hawkins (2012) highlight the importance of making the goal specific, observable, and measurable in their article "Opportunities to Respond: A Key Component of Effective Instruction." An example of such a goal would be to provide three opportunities to respond per minute for a fifteen-minute period during a tenth-grade U.S. history lesson on the War of 1812.

In addition to considering adding more OTRs into your lesson plan, you may want to think about ways students can respond (such as hand signals, unison response, or written response). Additionally, you may want to consider an instructional activity that includes a high rate of OTRs (such as about mathematics facts in a mathematics unit, reading comprehension questions in an English language arts unit, significant names or dates in a history unit, or steps in a life cycle in a science unit). Certain subjects and approaches to subjects better lend themselves to this strategy than others do. Teachers can also think about ways to self-reinforce their own daily goals so they meet them!

Implement the Action Plan

Once the teacher has created a goal for increasing OTRs and has created a lesson that easily lends itself to OTRs, the teacher is ready to implement this strategy. The teacher asks the entire class a question requiring a response. Students can give a choral response, or they can have response cards at their desks. Once you have delivered the opportunity to respond, you can make a tally mark for each response on a clipboard or on the lesson plan sheet with OTR questions written on it. Although you are delivering OTRs at a quick pace, you must provide three seconds of wait time to respond (Haydon et al., 2012).

To begin, you should have a goal of providing students with a minimum of three OTRs per minute. It is important to remember to use student responses as a quick way to assess students' understanding of instruction, which helps you know who is getting the material and who needs additional instruction or more support.

Monitor and Adjust the Plan as Necessary

During the implementation process, the teacher needs to self-monitor while delivering OTRs (Haydon et al., 2012). You can graph the information gleaned on your rate of delivery to visualize the progress you are making toward your self-selected OTR goal. Again, either another teacher, an administrator, or a mentor can do the monitoring, or you can choose to self-monitor. When you are first increasing your rate of OTRs, it may be better to have someone else monitor your progress. The action plan continues, and adjustments can be made as needed based on data collected. You can fade self-management and additional supports when data indicate you have met your goal. For example, a teacher who has met an OTR goal for five consecutive days may want to think about self-monitoring weekly rather than daily with the ultimate goal of fading self-monitoring completely.

Figure 7.1 shows an action plan to increase the rate of opportunities to respond.

Step 1: Determine the Present Use of Opportunities to Respond
Who is collecting data?

Ms. Rochester (teacher) and Ms. Dennis (mentor teacher)

☑ Another person is collecting data: _____

☑ I am collecting my own data.

How are data collected?

☐ Counter

☑ Tally mark

☐ Other: _____

Current rate of opportunities to respond (OTRs): 0.53

Day 1: Number of OTRs / minute = rate
9 OTRs in 15 minutes = 0.60

Day 2: Number of OTRs / minute = rate
14 OTRs in 15 minutes = 0.93

Day 3: Number of OTRs / minute = rate
28 OTRs in 15 minutes = 1.87

Day 4: Number of OTRs / minute = rate
40 OTRs in 15 minutes = 2.67

Day 5: Number of OTRs / minute = rate
45 OTRs in 15 minutes = 3.0

My current average rate of OTRs is _____.

Step 2: Plan for Increasing Opportunities to Respond

My goal is to increase my rate of opportunities to respond to an average of
_____ per minute.

What types of opportunities to respond will you use? List specific examples.

1. Thumbs-up or thumbs-down

2. Responses written on whiteboards

3. Responses said out loud

4. Response cards with A, B, C, and D

Will you make changes to instruction or add activities? List examples.

1. I will add the type of opportunity to respond to my teacher notes.

2. I will make sure to explain my expectations to students when responding.

3. I will make sure I have all my supplies ready prior to beginning.

4. I will create questions where students are able to use the response cards
   with A, B, C, and D.

Step 3: Implement, Monitor, and Adjust the Plan

Current rate of OTRs:

Day 1: Number of OTRs / minute = rate
45 OTRs in 15 minutes = 3.0

Day 2: Number of OTRs / minute = rate
45 OTRs in 15 minutes = 3.0

Day 3: Number of OTRs / minute = rate
60 OTRs in 15 minutes = 4.0

Day 4: Number of OTRs / minute = rate
60 OTRs in 15 minutes = 4.0

Day 5: Number of OTRs / minute = rate
60 OTRs in 15 minutes = 4.0

What adjustments need to be made?

It helped having everything written in my lesson plan. At first, I was forgetting,
but having my lesson plan with notes really helped. It also helped explaining
my expectations to my students and making sure they had all their materials.
The lesson was fun because the students were so involved in what we
were doing.

Figure 7.1: Opportunities-to-respond action plan.

*Visit **go.SolutionTree.com/behavior** for a free reproducible version of this figure.*

Review Ideas for Reinforcement

As we mentioned previously, all students should receive positive reinforcement; however, students with challenging behaviors need to hear that they can be as successful in the classroom as their peers who do not exhibit challenging behaviors (Scheuermann & Hall, 2016). Reinforcement (for example, verbal praise and positive affirmation) strengthens the relationships among the teacher and students. Specifically related to OTRs, the teacher can consistently verbally reinforce students after they respond to questions, regardless of the accuracy of the answers.

Let's see an example of Ms. Lumpkins offering this kind of reinforcement.

> Caleb, a student who exhibits inattentiveness during science class, correctly answers a particular question about the periodic table on a homework assignment. However, when Ms. Lumpkins asks Caleb the same question during class, he is distracted and answers incorrectly. She gives a clear, quick, and simple correction and then repeats the question, allowing Caleb to provide the correct answer. Caleb gives the correct answer, and Ms. Lumpkins promptly gives Caleb verbal praise.

In addition to offering verbal reinforcement to individual students, as Ms. Lumpkins does in the preceding scenario, the teacher may provide a whole-group reinforcement (for example, five minutes of free time at the end of class, or extra recess time) to the entire class after the OTR instructional time. You can reinforce OTRs in other ways, including with tangible reinforcers, such as stickers. You can also always allow the students to choose the type of positive reinforcement they desire after completing the classroom assignment; positive reinforcements may include screen time, free time to read or listen to music, time to complete outside classwork, or time to socialize with their peers. When students frequently receive reinforcement, they are more likely to be engaged during the instruction.

Consider Cultural and Linguistic Diversity

Using students' preferred names and pronouncing their names correctly are integral components to implementing OTRs (Tualaulelei, 2021). Every day in classrooms around the world, names are used as personal identifiers, and it is inevitable that teachers will occasionally encounter names they are unfamiliar with or perceive as difficult to pronounce. Culturally responsive educators respect and honor students' names (Marrun, 2018). When teachers mispronounce or anglicize names, or assign easier-to-pronounce names to students of color, for example, they convey to their students that their racial, ethnic, cultural, and linguistic diversity is unimportant in the classroom.

The practices of not calling students by the names they prefer to be called and mispronouncing their names frame diverse students with non-Eurocentric names as needing to be "fixed" or "helped" so that they will fit in and assimilate with the majority culture. In her article for *Taboo: The Journal of Culture and Education* on this topic, Norma A. Marrun (2018) recounts her reluctance to ask her teachers to call her by her middle name, which her family used at home:

> As a child, my family instilled the importance of respecting my elders; this included my teachers. Within the Latino community, children are taught to respect their teachers and questioning or correcting a teacher is a sign of disrespect and an indication of one's family failure to raise *un hijo bien educado* (a child that is well educated; Delgado-Gaitan, 1992; Valdés, 1996). . . . I would not have corrected my teacher even if I had been fluent in English because I was taught not to question her authority and to respect the values of the school. Respect for teachers in the Latino community prevents many students and their families from questioning teachers for (re)naming their children. Although I preferred to be called by my middle name Angelica, my teachers called me by my first name Norma because that was how I was listed on the class roster. (p. 8)

At the beginning of each school year, and when any new students join your classroom, make sure you ask students what names they prefer to be called, and also make sure you are pronouncing their names correctly.

When implementing OTRs, be intentional in eliciting participation from all students equally. Nationwide research conducted in U.S. public and private school classrooms over several years has consistently found that beginning in elementary school, teachers ask female students fewer questions, engage less frequently with them, and provide male students with more feedback (Andrus, Jacobs, & Kuriloff, 2018; Herbel-Eisenmann & Shah, 2019).

Inequities in student engagement extend to students from diverse racial and ethnic backgrounds. Students of color may have few teacher-student interactions and experience treatment based on negative racial stereotypes (Leath, Mathews, Harrison, & Chavous, 2019). Further, Black and Latinx students are historically underrepresented in gifted and talented programs and Advanced Placement classes (Xu, Solanki, & Fink, 2021).

In order to support the active engagement of *all* students, it is imperative that you develop a system to make sure you equally extend OTRs to all students. The following ideas will help ensure all students have equal opportunities to participate.

- Use a seating chart, and place a tally mark next to a student's name after you have called on the student. This way, you can keep track of the OTR questions you present to each student. If a student does not know the answer, allow the student a few seconds of wait time; then allow the student to "phone a friend" for help with the answer.

- Write each student's name on a wooden craft stick. Place the sticks in a cup. After asking a question, draw a stick out of the cup. Once a student answers correctly, remove that stick from the cup. Do this until all students have answered correctly.

Incorporate Student Interests

There are many ways to incorporate OTRs in the classroom, and trying different things is in itself engaging because students are so active while they are learning. It is important that the teacher use a variety of strategies for student responses (for example, choral response, thumbs-up or thumbs-down, response cards, and technology). Students will have their favorite type of response, but all students may not have the same favorite. Using different mechanisms for student responses will help ensure you meet all students' interests. Students can even create their own response card set with their preferred materials or favorite colors. You can use the student interest inventories discussed in previous chapters to find books, topics, and materials that match students' interests to the subject matter being taught.

EXAMPLES OF HOW TO UTILIZE OPPORTUNITIES TO RESPOND

The following examples can be used at the elementary and secondary levels. While these examples are fairly low tech, you can use websites such as Kahoot! (https://kahoot.com) for higher-tech options. Students can respond using technology such as tablet computers and clickers.

- When you ask students to recall previously learned information, provide small whiteboards for students to quickly write down their answers. Students can then each hold up their board to show their answer.

- When you want to ask a group of students multiple-choice questions, first create double-sided cards with *yes* or *no*, *true* or *false*, *agree* or *disagree*, *A* or *B*, and so on appearing on the two sides. Students can hold up a card so the correct answer faces you.

- When you engage students to determine whether they agree or disagree with an answer, have students show a thumbs-up or thumbs-down to agree or disagree.

- When you would like to hear the same response from all students, you can utilize choral responses.

Now that we have gone through how providing OTRs is an evidence-based practice, and we have detailed how to effectively implement higher rates of OTRs during teacher-led instruction, we need to revisit our scenario with Ms. Lumpkins.

Ms. Lumpkins finds that increasing her rate of OTRs is a highly effective strategy for her students' academic success and motivation in the classroom. Ms. Lumpkins varies the ways she implements OTRs. She implements this strategy for the whole group and individual students. She also provides multiple ways for her students to respond to her academic inquiries.

As a whole-group example, Ms. Lumpkins is teaching her students the Latin and Greek affixes and roots of words to her entire class. She creates individual Elkonin boxes (three blank squares) and distributes them to each student. Next, Ms. Lumpkins displays the Latin or Greek root of the word on the classroom's whiteboard (for example, *aqua* or *bio*). She instructs the students to use the Elkonin boxes to place the root word in the first box, write a definition in the second, and then provide examples in the third.

When the students are finished, Ms. Lumpkins asks them to share their results. She gives verbal praise and feedback as appropriate. Ms. Lumpkins specifically reinforces every student for his, her, or their contributions. Ms. Lumpkins then prompts a whole-group discussion about the class's progress on this concept. Ms. Lumpkins often has her students utilize response cards, hand gestures, clickers, and whiteboards to elicit their responses in class.

As an individual student example, Ms. Lumpkins distributes a vocabulary root word activity for all students to complete independently since her students are learning about Greek and Latin affixes and root words. As they are working on this activity, Ms. Lumpkins circulates around the classroom and verbally reinforces students for their work. In addition, she asks questions of various individual students. Finally, after all students have completed their activity, Ms. Lumpkins asks the class specific questions about this activity.

Since she previously walked around the classroom during their independent work time, she knows specific students will answer her questions correctly. She calls on these students to answer her questions related to the activity. Ms. Lumpkins asks the class to raise their hands if they agree with the answer given by the student she called on and to give thumbs-down if they disagree. She verbally reinforces all students with a positive comment for their effort on the activity.

We have provided you with detailed information on how to actively engage all your students through the evidence-based strategy of opportunities to respond during teacher-directed lessons. In table 7.1, we provide you with a short list of dos and don'ts for implementing high rates of opportunities to respond in the classroom.

Table 7.1: Dos and Don'ts for Opportunities to Respond

Do	Don't
✓ Have students utilize technology when implementing OTRs.	✗ Provide students with software or apps for OTRs without first training them on the technology.
✓ Make sure you reinforce students immediately after their responses.	✗ Wait too long to respond.
✓ Call on reluctant students only when you are confident they have the correct response.	✗ Use OTRs to catch students who may not be paying attention or are otherwise off task.
✓ Provide prompts and support to lead students to the correct answer.	✗ Criticize incorrect responses.
✓ Provide several seconds of wait time for students to respond.	✗ Expect an immediate response.

CONCLUDING THOUGHTS

Increasing the rate of opportunities to respond to teacher-directed questions is a tier 1 evidence-based strategy that teachers use to actively engage students in their learning (Van Camp et al., 2020). OTRs have been shown to improve student behavior and academic achievement because students receive additional chances to practice academic skills, which, in turn, leads to increased academic engagement, fewer class disruptions, and decreased challenging behaviors. Opportunities to respond naturally provide positive reinforcement, which also promotes positive outcomes (MacSuga-Gage & Simonsen, 2015). Although effectively monitoring and planning for OTRs take effort on the teacher's part, the effort is worth it because of the positive outcomes that come from it.

Next, we provide reflective questions to ask yourself as you are implementing higher rates of opportunities to respond during teacher-directed lessons in your classroom. In the appendix (page 165), we have provided resources you can consult as you implement the OTR strategy.

Chapter 7: Questions for Reflection

Write your responses to the following questions. Keep these responses in mind as you work to address challenging student behaviors and guide your students toward academic engagement and motivated learning.

1. Can you see yourself implementing opportunities to respond within your classroom? Why or why not?

2. Describe what you believe the biggest obstacles could be when implementing opportunities to respond with your students. What could you do to overcome the obstacles?

3. Describe what you believe the biggest benefits could be when implementing opportunities to respond with your students.

4. What are some potential reinforcers that you can use in your classroom to support your students while implementing opportunities to respond?

5. What system could you put into place to ensure you call on all students equally?

6. What method would you prefer to use when implementing opportunities to respond? Examples include response cards, digital responses, and choral responses.

7. Think of an activity or subject area where you would like to try to use opportunities to respond. How will you engage your students in opportunities to respond, and what questions will you ask?

8. How will you pair students to best promote academic and social growth in each student?

9. After implementing opportunities to respond in your classroom, consider this: Did you have any challenges?

10. Thinking about the challenges, what adjustments or changes could be made to make opportunities to respond work better for you?

Chapter 8

Remember What You Talked About: A Guide to Precorrection

Mr. MaGehee has been teaching a middle-grades computer discovery class for three years and knows to review his classroom rules and procedures with his students during the first few weeks of school. However, he has noticed his students often become restless and noncompliant around the fifth or sixth week. Many educators affectionately refer to this time period as the "student honeymoon coming to an end." Even though Mr. MaGehee continues to review his classroom rules and procedures with his students during this time, he also increases positive reinforcement (for example, verbal praise and extended free computer time) with his class. However, he knows he needs other strategies to help him combat his students' challenging behaviors (such as talking, not completing work, and visiting websites not related to academic tasks) and increase motivation.

Mr. MaGehee decides to dig into his old college notes from his teacher-preparation program and comes across a strategy called *precorrection*. His notes read that precorrection is simply reminding his students or one particular student of appropriate behavior before they can make an error. Mr. MaGehee decides to add this strategy coupled with positive reinforcement to his classroom management plan. He believes that the reminder his students receive from precorrection and specific positive reinforcement will motivate them during this challenging time of the school year.

School officials (teachers, paraprofessionals, and administrators) sometimes take a reactionary approach to discipline by waiting for students to engage in inappropriate behavior and then providing a consequence (Ennis, Lane, Menzies, & Owens, 2018). Finding proactive approaches before challenges occur can be extremely beneficial to teachers and students. Mr. MaGehee, from the scenario, is excited to implement precorrection with his students because he wants to focus on being positive rather than pointing out the negative behaviors. With precorrection, teachers spend less time correcting problem behaviors while students experience fewer negative interactions with adults at school. Although consequences are still needed when inappropriate behaviors occur, focusing on proactive measures can improve the school climate by reducing the number of challenging behaviors that occur in the first place.

Precorrection is a low-intensity, proactive strategy designed to prevent predictable difficult behaviors by influencing the classroom environment and increasing the chances of desirable behaviors (Ennis et al., 2018). Preventable predictable behaviors may include students getting out of their seats without asking, talking when the teacher is talking, not following directions the first time they are given, and not using classroom materials for their intended purpose.

If students are doing independent work while the teacher is working with a small group of students, the teacher can say, prior to working with the small group, "Remember when you are doing your independent work, you are staying in your seat. If you have a question, you can quietly, in a whisper voice, ask your neighbor. If your neighbor does not know the answer to your question, please raise one finger, which signals me that you have a question. I know you will do a great job of staying in your seats while you do independent work!" While students are working independently and the teacher is working with the small group, the teacher can compliment the class for working so hard.

As a teacher, you may remind students that you are looking for them to not talk and to have their eyes on you while you are talking: "I am going to explain the directions of our assignment. Before I explain, I want all voices turned off and all eyes on me so that you are ready to listen to what I am going to tell you."

To precorrect for following directions the first time they are given, you may find it helpful to have the directions on the board or on a piece of paper so students can easily follow along. You must explicitly teach the directions to be followed so students know what the directions actually are. Prior to allowing students to use materials, for example, remind the students how they should use the materials (such as, "We walk rather than run with scissors in our hands," and "Scissors are meant only for cutting paper").

Teachers can implement precorrection across all settings for students at any age and ability (Evanovich & Kern, 2018). They can use it schoolwide or even with individual students or groups in addressing both academic behaviors (such as improved on-task behaviors) and social behaviors (such as reduced aggression). In their systematic review of the literature on precorrection, researchers Robin Parks Ennis, David James Royer, Kathleen Lynne Lane, and Claire E. Griffith (2017) examine research articles on situations where precorrection has been implemented in prekindergarten through twelfth grade and used over a period of time. They find precorrection to be an evidence-based practice in elementary and secondary settings. This research shows that when precorrection is implemented, challenging student behaviors decrease (Ennis et al., 2017). Overall, research shows precorrection decreases the amount of time spent correcting and redirecting, prevents repetition of inappropriate behaviors, and increases opportunities for students to receive positive feedback and reinforcement of preferred behaviors during interactions with teachers (Evanovich & Kern, 2018).

This chapter shows how to implement precorrection by identifying the context in which challenging behaviors occur and how to change that context to promote more positive behaviors. It also shows teachers how to delineate for students expected, appropriate behaviors and to develop plans for students to enact these expected behaviors. The chapter wraps up with a Concluding Thoughts section and a reproducible page that includes reflective questions to ponder. The chapter will revisit the Mr. MaGehee scenario throughout to make the concepts of the chapter visible within an imaginary school context.

HOW TO IMPLEMENT PRECORRECTION

To start thinking about how to implement precorrection, let's consider Mr. MaGehee's computer class and how he might use precorrection with his students. When Mr. MaGehee's students enter the room and sit down, they often talk to each other instead of logging on to their computers, which goes against his classroom rules and procedures. Rather than waiting to correct students who do not comply with this procedure, Mr. MaGehee can use precorrection. He reminds the students, as they are walking into class, to log on to the computer and go to the website written on the board to get ready for the lesson. He then gives individual incentive points to students who comply. Let's see what Mr. MaGehee's use of precorrection looks like with Tricia, a student who often logs on to YouTube rather than completing classwork.

> Once students sit down, Mr. MaGehee walks over to Tricia and makes the simple statement, "When you log on to your computer, what will you do?" This question prompts Tricia to say, "I will go to the website on the board." At this point, Mr. MaGehee gives specific praise for correctly stating expectations. He also tells Tricia he looks forward to coming back around to see her on the correct website so she can earn individual incentive points.
>
> Mr. MaGehee walks away to talk to other students. He comes back a few minutes later to provide Tricia with an incentive point for complying with the precorrection request.

In situations such as the preceding example, you shouldn't wait too long to check on whether the student implemented the appropriate behavior, because you want the student to be successful and earn the incentive points.

This sort of simple precorrection is grounded in the seminal work of Geoffrey Colvin, George Sugai, and Bill Patching (1993), who recommend a seven-step plan to assist teachers in proactively addressing problem behavior using precorrection (as cited in Evanovich & Kern, 2018). We use that seven-step plan, along with the additional step of considering cultural and linguistic diversity, as the basis for implementing the precorrection strategy. The strategy steps are as follows.

1. **Identify the context and predictable challenging behaviors:** In this step, teachers identify patterns of challenging student behaviors by observing how certain behaviors are tied to specific environments and activities.

2. **Define the desired behaviors:** Once teachers establish the contexts for challenging behaviors, they use this step to articulate which behaviors they would like to see instead in the contexts they previously identified.

3. **Adjust the environment to promote student success:** Teachers use this step to guide them in adjusting environmental factors to promote positive behaviors.

4. **Provide opportunities for students to practice desired behaviors:** This step shows teachers how to practice desired behaviors with students by providing examples and nonexamples of the behaviors.

5. **Provide the preferred reinforcement when students engage in the desired behaviors:** This step guides teachers in selecting and offering reinforcements that students like.

6. **Develop a plan for prompting students to engage in the preferred behaviors:** Students may need extra reminders to engage in desired behaviors. This helps teachers prompt students to meet that need.

7. **Create a progress-monitoring plan to determine the precorrection plan's effectiveness:** Teachers use this step to collect data on whether the precorrection strategy is effective and to make adjustments if necessary.

8. **Consider cultural and linguistic diversity:** This step helps teachers ensure equity by showing them ways to communicate with students about the strategy in ways that honor diverse communication styles.

Identify the Context and Predictable Challenging Behaviors

First, the teacher needs to identify the cause of the behaviors of concern (Evanovich & Kern, 2018). Specifically, what is the predictable challenging behavior, and when does the behavior occur? Understanding the context is important for the teacher to be able to correct behaviors before they actually occur.

The challenging behavior is predictable because the student exhibits the behavior almost every time or every time within a specific context. It may be a specific class, a specific subject, or even a particular time of day. For instance, Mr. MaGehee's students particularly exhibit the challenging behavior when they transition to class and log on to their computers. The context may be different for different students and different teachers, but it is always regular and predictable. For instance, Mrs. Phillips, a fifth-grade teacher, may identify challenging behaviors when students transition from one class to another in the hallway. The students may run and push each other, particularly if they have to wait for their next teacher to be ready. Their voice level may be too high.

Define the Desired Behaviors

The teacher should define a desired (or expected) behavior that is appropriate to the situation, and the teacher should have a clear reason why the behavior is desired (Evanovich & Kern, 2018). Examples and nonexamples can be helpful when sharing the plan. For example, a student of yours may run to be at the front of the line although the appropriate behavior is walking to get in the line. When defining the desired behavior, you need to do so as specifically as possible. You want to state exactly what the behavior looks like. Rather than saying, "Don't run in the hall," you need to say, "Walk in the hall."

For instance, a teacher like Mrs. Phillips may decide to focus on eliminating shouting in the halls. She may also want to focus on a particular student, Alex, who gets too close to other students. Mrs. Phillips defines the expected behavior of students standing in the hallway as closing one's mouth and not making noises. Examples include completely sealing one's lips (touching without gaps) and not using one's voice (or vocal cords) in any way. Nonexamples include making noises such as whistling or humming, talking, and shouting.

Mrs. Phillips collects data on the number of times she has to correct students for their voice level being too loud. Across five days of baseline data, she corrects students an average of fifteen times. She retains this information to determine whether her subsequent efforts have an impact.

Adjust the Environment to Promote Student Success

Once the expected behaviors have been identified, the teacher adjusts the context (for example, the activity or the setting) by changing what happens before the behavior occurs within the setting, context, or task (Evanovich & Kern, 2018). Adjusting small things ahead of time can decrease challenging behaviors. For example, making changes to the context may include adjusting the following.

- **Teacher behaviors:** Teachers may adjust their behavior by walking around the classroom rather than sitting at their desk or by writing on the SMART Board rather than on the projector.

- **The instruction or activity:** Instructional adjustments may include small-group rather than large-group instruction. Rather than completing a worksheet for a mathematics book, students could receive the activity in a different format.

- **Preferential seating:** A student's seat can move to a spot closer to the teacher or away from a particular student.

- **The means of instruction:** Maybe a student would prefer to listen to an audio version of a text rather than reading it independently.

The examples provided here are just that—examples. There are many different ways to adjust the environment to help students be more successful. For instance, Mrs. Phillips talks to her colleague Mrs. Miller about how they can better coordinate their time so the students are not waiting in the hall for long between classes. Mrs. Phillips also decides to have students line up based on their assigned seats in her class, and she decides she is better off walking the halls where students wait than standing at her door. Through these changes, Mrs. Phillips adjusts the environment to help her students be more successful.

Provide Opportunities for Students to Practice Desired Behaviors

The best way for the teacher to engage students in the desired new behaviors is to give them opportunities to practice these expected behaviors (Evanovich & Kern, 2018). The teacher might explicitly teach the student a lesson based on steps 2 and 3 (page 148) with embedded opportunities to respond. Practicing in this way allows the teacher to monitor students' accuracy in performing the desired or expected behavior.

Mrs. Phillips might explicitly teach the hallway expectations during the transition time. She could provide students examples and nonexamples. For example, she could demonstrate to the students walking versus running in the hall or talking to the person next to her versus standing quietly. Before doing anything new, Mrs. Phillips explicitly teaches the students what her expectations are. As a class, they go over examples of what the desired behaviors look like and what they don't look like. Doing this helps ensure students truly understand her expectations.

Mrs. Phillips could also ask Alex, the student who often has the most challenging behaviors, to demonstrate for her and the class. She might ask Alex to demonstrate desired hallway procedures during a time when he is on task. She wants him to have a positive interaction by getting to be a leader. She can then positively reinforce him by verbally praising him while he is providing an example. Having Alex show the class also gives him practice in completing desired hallway procedures. This is intended to be a positive experience and not a negative one where the student feels called out.

Provide the Preferred Reinforcement When Students Engage in the Desired Behaviors

After the teacher has explicitly taught the desired behavior, students receive reinforcement for completing the behavior (Evanovich & Kern, 2018). The reinforcement needs to match the students' interests and needs to offer them a stronger appeal than whatever reinforcement they receive when they display the inappropriate behaviors (such as attention or a prime place in line). When you figure out what the preferred reinforcement is, you are more likely to see student success.

Mrs. Phillips, for example, provides specific praise for desired behaviors. She also uses her ticket system so students can earn, as a class, free time at the end of class to play their favorite mathematics computer game.

Develop a Plan for Prompting Students to Engage in the Preferred Behaviors

The teacher creates a plan for a student who may have more challenging needs and require additional reminders to show the expected or desired behaviors (Evanovich & Kern, 2018). Prompts may include using proximity control, pointing, or verbally stating the prompt ("Remember to walk in the hall"). It is important to remember that the prompt must match students' developmental needs.

Mrs. Phillips decides to use the verbal prompt, "Remember, as we go into the hallway, we are fifth-grade leaders. Our voices should be off and our lips sealed." She also uses the visual cue of putting her finger on her lips. Mrs. Phillips stands next to Alex and looks directly at him with her finger to her lips to encourage him to show the desired behavior. She provides specific praise to Alex and gives the class tickets for demonstrating the desired behavior.

Create a Progress-Monitoring Plan to Determine the Precorrection Plan's Effectiveness

The teacher must collect data on the occurrence of desired behaviors to determine whether the intervention should continue or if the precorrection plan needs to undergo changes (Evanovich & Kern, 2018). Data collection may include observations before and after implementation of precorrection to track how often the behavior occurs. Data help you know whether what you are doing is working. They can also help you know where you may need to make adjustments for the students to be more successful.

Mrs. Phillips collects data to determine whether her use of precorrection works for her students. She collects data for five days by counting the number of times she corrects inappropriate voice levels. The average number of times she corrects behaviors each day is three. Mrs. Phillips determines precorrection was an effective strategy for her to use.

When teachers implement an intervention such as precorrection with fidelity, they can make appropriate decisions about the intervention's impact on a targeted behavior. Researchers Lauren L. Evanovich and Laura Kern (2018) created a treatment-fidelity checklist allowing for teachers to collect, monitor, and modify data as needed. The checklist can include space for notes and examples and nonexamples of direct behavior. Figure 8.1 shows how Mr. MaGehee can complete the treatment-fidelity checklist in our chapter-opening scenario with his class.

Precorrection Treatment-Fidelity Checklist

Student: Tricia Miranda

Setting: Computer lab

Observer: Mr. MaGehee

Observation time: 11:00–11:30 a.m.

Yes = 1; no = 0

| Step 1: | Has the predictable behavior been identified? | ① | 0 |
| | Has the context where the predictable behavior occurs been identified? | ① | 0 |

Predictable challenging behavior: I have identified my student's challenging behavior as getting on YouTube rather than beginning the computer assignment posted on the board.

Setting and context: The behavior occurs when students are walking into the room and completing independent work on the computer in the computer lab.

| Step 2: | Have the desired and expected behaviors been defined? | ① | 0 |

Desired and expected behaviors: I defined the desired behavior of quietly walking into the computer lab and logging on to the computer. Once logged on to the computer, the student will look at the board and begin completing the assignment listed on the board.

Nonexamples: Nonexamples include not logging on to the computer as well as logging on to the computer and going to YouTube to watch videos.

| Step 3: | Have the setting and context been adapted to promote student success? | ① | 0 |

Setting and context modifications: After I teach the desired behavior, I will greet students at the door rather than staying at my desk. When most students are in the room, I will walk around the room and monitor computer activity.

| Step 4: | Has the student been given opportunities to practice the desired and expected behaviors? | ① | 0 |

Opportunities to practice: First, I will review my expectations with all the students. My expectations are for all students to quietly walk into the classroom, put their backpack on the back of their chair, log on to the computer, look at the board for the independent assignment to complete, and begin working. As a class, we will go over examples and nonexamples. Because Tricia has the hardest time with this task, I will have her model the expected behaviors. Modeling expected behaviors allows her additional practice and positive peer and teacher attention. I will have all students practice the desired behavior of entering the room quietly and completing the work posted on the board.

Figure 8.1: Completed precorrection treatment-fidelity checklist. *continued →*

Step 5:	Has the student received reinforcement for demonstrating expected behaviors?	①	0

Reinforcement system based on students' interests: I will provide specific praise when students are completing their computer work. I will provide Tricia with specific praise for logging on to the correct site once she logs on to the computer. We have a ticket system in the class. Students who comply with the expected behaviors will receive tickets. The class has specific items they can purchase with their tickets. Tricia has her own system where she can earn YouTube time by purchasing computer minutes with her tickets.

Step 6:	Has a plan for prompting been created to engage the student in desired and expected behaviors?	①	0

Plan for prompting: I will prompt students as they are walking into the classroom to check the board for where they need to begin. When Tricia walks into the room, I will give her a paper that has the specific site where she needs to begin. I will be walking around the room providing prompts and praise as students comply. As Tricia is able to walk into the room and look at the board for the website to go to, the individualized paper can be faded.

Step 7:	Has a progress-monitoring plan been developed to determine the effectiveness of precorrection?	①	0

Progress-monitoring plan: I will have a tally sheet and make a mark on the sheet for each time Tricia needs to be corrected. I will collect baseline data prior to beginning precorrection. The number of tally marks Tricia receives on the sheet should decrease. Additionally, I will graph the tally marks at the end of the week. The graph should show a decrease if precorrection is working to improve Tricia's desired behavior.

Total $N = 8$

$N/(8) \times 100 = 100$ percent

*Visit **go.SolutionTree.com/behavior** for a free reproducible version of this figure.*

Consider Cultural and Linguistic Diversity

Teachers engage in culturally responsive classroom management strategies and practices when they establish expectations, explicitly communicate them, and carry them out in an equitable manner (Gaias, Johnson, Bottiani, Debnam, & Bradshaw, 2019). Explicit teaching of classroom rules is consistently found to be a key determinant of effective classroom management (Alter & Haydon, 2017).

Author Calli recalls her first year of teaching middle school. Her classroom was far from being a well-managed environment. Meanwhile, the teacher in the class across the hall did have a very well-managed classroom. It turned out that the teacher's key to success was explicitly teaching her classroom procedures every day for the first six weeks of school and reteaching them after the winter break. This strategy also proved to be very effective for the author. Explicit teaching is crucial, as social norms and expectations vary from culture to culture and also from teacher to teacher. When students have a clear understanding of exactly what is expected of them, they are more likely to meet those expectations!

As you are engaging in precorrection, learn about differences in communication styles between your culture and that of your students (Larson, Pas, Bradshaw, Rosenberg, & Day-Vines, 2018). For example, is eye contact between children or youth and their parents or older individuals expected, or is it interpreted as defiance? The following examples are broad generalizations of differences in communication styles and approaches. No culture is a monolith, however; that is to say, these concepts will vary widely from person to person within the same racial or ethnic group (Grothe, 2020). Consider how the following differences may affect communication between you and your students when using precorrection.

- Silence:
  - In many Asian cultures—in Japan (Akechi et al., 2013) and Korea (Cho, 2004), for example—silence is valued as a sign of respect. When differences of opinion arise, people opt for silence, rather than saying something that would offend the other person (Grothe, 2020).

  - In some cultures, such as in some Asian and Nordic cultures, silence is preferred to speaking when an individual encounters a new or unexpected event.

  - In cultures such as some of those in West Africa, in which power and importance belong to older individuals, those in power carry the responsibility of speaking while those not in power are expected to remain quiet.

  - In some Native American cultures, silence carries specific connotations. In Navajo culture, for example, long periods of silence can be preferred over small talk (Bennett & Fitzwater, 2010). Members of the Lakota tribes may use silence to convey disagreement (Kalbfleisch, 2009).

- Verbal expression:
    - In some Western cultures, including in the United States, verbal communication and freedom of expression are highly valued.
- Elaborate expression:
    - Individuals who use this style use many words, descriptors, and comparisons.
    - Rich, expressive language is used in everyday conversations.
    - Individuals from Latinx, African, and Arab cultures often utilize elaborate expression.
- Understated expression:
    - Cultures that value understated expression value simplicity over details.
    - Individuals who utilize few words may be considered more trustworthy than individuals who use a lot of words.
    - In Amish and many Asian cultures, the preferred style of communication is often understated expression.

To learn more about and see additional examples of cultural differences in body language, we suggest reviewing *When Cultures Collide: Leading Across Cultures* by Richard D. Lewis (2018) and "Body Language Around the World" by Kris Rugsaken (2006). Business Insider (2015) also provides a useful online infographic illustrating cultural body-language differences derived from Lewis's (2006) work, among other sources (visit https://tinyurl.com/3xxrubk3).

Keep cultural differences in mind while communicating as directly as possible with students. Doing so will ensure that your instructions, procedures, policies, and so on are clear and will reduce the likelihood that they are misunderstood. For example, use this: "Remember, hands to yourself as you line up to go to the auditorium." Don't use this: "Can all of you please remember to keep your hands to yourself as we line up to go to the auditorium?" Also, you may use humor to communicate expectations. When using this approach, avoid sarcasm and irony (Ashman & Snow, 2019). Although both can be employed in some situations, you should avoid them in giving students directions in order to prevent misunderstandings.

EXAMPLES OF HOW TO UTILIZE PRECORRECTION

The following examples show how teachers can use precorrection in a variety of scenarios.

- Before you transition to the next activity or assignment, you might tell students, "In five minutes, we'll be starting our narrative final drafts. Please get your Chromebook out and open your essay."

- Before the bell rings, you might tell students, "Remember, when the bell rings, you will wait until I have dismissed you to go to your next class."

- When a student guesses at a word instead of using decoding skills, you might tell the student, "Remember, every letter makes a sound. Sound out the letters you see."

- When students enter the classroom after lunch, recess, and so on, you might tell the students, "When you enter the room, put your things away, and get out your mathematics notebook and pencil. Line up to sharpen your pencil if you need to."

We have gone through the steps to implement precorrection in the classroom. Let's return to our scenario to see how precorrection works for Mr. MaGehee and his students.

Mr. MaGehee provides precorrection examples for his entire class and individual students. Specifically, Mr. MaGehee has observed that transition times are difficult for his entire class. He decides to implement precorrection coupled with verbal praise to help rectify these challenges. Mr. MaGehee begins telling his class every day before the end-of-class bell rings, "The bell will ring in five minutes. Please remember to walk out of the class quietly and slowly." He also gives verbal praise to the entire class and specific students, when needed. Specifically, Mr. MaGehee says, "Thank you, class, for walking out of the classroom quietly."

Mr. MaGehee also has specific students who would benefit from precorrection. For example, Jake often has conflicts with his peers when they complete their weekly group project. He will monopolize the computer and not allow his group members to work on the project with him. Once Mr. MaGehee provides the class with specific group project directions, he walks to Jake's designated area and says, "Jake, it is important we all work together in a group on this week's project. Please allow your peers access to the computer when it is their turn." After Mr. MaGehee gives these precorrection directives to Jake and observes him chatting with his group about the project, he follows up with, "Jake, you are doing so well working together with your peers."

Now that we have gone into specific detail on how to implement the evidence-based strategy of precorrection, there are a few things we would like you to remember before you begin to plan. In table 8.1, we provide you with a short list of dos and don'ts for implementing precorrection in the classroom.

Table 8.1: Dos and Don'ts for Precorrection

Do	Don't
✓ Use humor.	✗ Use sarcasm.
✓ Learn about students' cultural norms related to communication.	✗ Demand eye contact.
✓ Increase use of precorrection when students return from long breaks.	✗ Expect students to be immediately compliant after returning to school from a break.
✓ Use direct instructions and directives.	✗ Only elicit reprimands when students do not exhibit the target behavior.
✓ Be succinct in your communication.	✗ Give long-winded, multistep directions.

CONCLUDING THOUGHTS

Precorrection is a preventive and proactive evidence-based strategy to implement with all students. Although precorrection is great for all students at tier 1, it can be particularly beneficial for students with challenging behaviors at tier 2. Precorrection allows you to prevent challenging behaviors from happening. All students are much more likely to do what you want them to do when you explicitly tell them what your expectations are.

Sometimes, teachers assume that students know what their teachers want, but this isn't always the case, particularly for students who have challenging behaviors. Set students up for success by letting them know what you expect ahead of time.

When you want to precorrect the behaviors of a particular student, it is important to identify the context and predictable challenging behaviors. The desired behaviors need to be defined. Then you can adjust the environment to promote student success. You need to make sure you provide students with the opportunity to practice and give them their preferred reinforcement when they engage in the desired behaviors. Developing a plan for collecting data and for prompting desired behaviors helps ensure student success. Data collection can also help you know how effective the plan is and what changes you need to make.

Next, we provide reflective questions to ask yourself as you are implementing precorrection. In the appendix (page 165), we have provided resources you can consult as you implement the precorrection strategy.

Chapter 8: Questions for Reflection

Write your responses to the following questions. Keep these responses in mind as you work to address challenging student behaviors and guide your students toward academic engagement and motivated learning.

1. Create a list of times when you believe your students would most benefit from precorrection.

2. What precorrection statements could you use during those times? List the statements.

3. Think about a student who could benefit from more specific precorrection. What times and statements would work specifically for that student?

4. Can you see yourself implementing precorrection within your classroom? Why or why not?

5. Describe what you believe the biggest obstacles could be when implementing precorrection with your students. What could you do to overcome the obstacles?

6. Describe what you believe the biggest benefits could be when implementing precorrection with your students.

7. Describe reinforcements that you could add when using precorrection.

8. After implementing precorrection in your classroom, answer this question: "What went well?"

9. Did you have any challenges implementing precorrection in your classroom? If so, what were they?

10. Thinking about the challenges, what adjustments or changes could make precorrection work better for you?

Epilogue

We hope after reading this book, you feel empowered and encouraged either because you are already using some of the strategies we have talked about or because you learned something new that you want to try! Maybe you previously tried one of the strategies but have now realized some adjustments could make the strategy better fit your needs. Our goal in writing this book was to help you find a way to decrease your K–12 students' disruptive, challenging classroom behaviors and increase their academic engagement by providing evidence-based strategies that are easy to understand and implement.

As you think about implementing the strategies you've read about, pick one of the strategies you gravitate toward most, and start there. It is also important to think about your students' behaviors and what strategy you believe will be a good match to start with. You don't need to add all the strategies to your teaching repertoire at one time, because that gets overwhelming! Start small and work your way to adding more. Also, remember it can take some time to iron out the kinks in what you are trying to do. What looks like a quick fix on paper can be more challenging in the real world. Give the strategy some time, and evaluate as you go. Remember, consistency is key. Give yourself time to see the effectiveness of each strategy, perhaps a few weeks. Use this time to think about what is working well and what is not working well. You can adjust from there. Don't forget to give yourself a little grace when you are trying something new!

Thank you for taking the time to read our book. We truly hope we have made a positive impact on you and your students. Now go out there and be your amazing self!

Appendix

Resources for Teachers

This appendix lists books, websites, articles, and fact sheets that highlight practical information related to the chapters in this book. These resources are available for educators to learn more about each evidence-based practice. We believe this information will help readers build their knowledge base with regard to each practice we've discussed.

CHAPTER 1: CHALLENGING BEHAVIORS

The following books, articles, and online resources will help readers continue to build their understanding of the factors that influence challenging behaviors and the importance of educating students with challenging behaviors within the classroom.

Books

- *Beyond Versus: The Struggle to Understand the Interaction of Nature and Nurture* by James Tabery (2014)

- *The First Days of School: How to Be an Effective Teacher* by Harry K. Wong and Rosemary T. Wong (2018)

Articles

- "Breaking Down Barriers and Building Bridges: Transformative Practices in Community- and School-Based Urban Teacher Preparation" by Robert E. Lee (2018)

- "Creating a Positive Classroom Climate for Diversity" by Juan C. Garibay (2015)

- "Simple Strategies to Develop Rapport With Students and Build a Positive Classroom Climate" by Melissa Parks (2017)

- "Instructional Strategies to Help Online Students Learn: Feedback From Online Students" by Firm Faith Watson, Marianne Castano Bishop, and Debra Ferdinand-James (2017)

Online Resources

- The Center on Positive Behavioral Interventions and Supports website (www.pbis.org)

- "Building (and Maintaining) Rapport in the Classroom" (Smith, n.d.; www.depts.ttu.edu/tlpdc/Resources/Teaching_resources/TLPDC _teaching_resources/Documents/Building_Rapport_new.pdf)

CHAPTER 2: PROVIDING CHOICES

The following resources for providing choices will help readers continue to build their understanding of the importance of this evidence-based practice within the classroom. This book offers choice as a practical practice to use with students. The books, articles, and online resources listed here also show the use of choices as an important practice within the classroom.

Books

- *Learning to Choose, Choosing to Learn: The Key to Student Motivation and Achievement* by Mike Anderson (2016)

- *Just Ask Us: Kids Speak Out on Student Engagement* by Heather Wolpert-Gawron (2018)

Articles

- "Choice-Based Stimulus Preference Assessment for Children With or At-Risk for Emotional Disturbance in Educational Settings" by Seth A. King and Douglas E. Kostewicz (2014)

- "Educator 'What-Ifs': The Feasibility of Choice Making in the Classroom" by Kristine Jolivette, Robin Parks Ennis, and Nicole Cain Swoszowski (2017)

- "Academic Choice for Included Students With Emotional and Behavioral Disorders" by Mandi Davis Skerbetz and Douglas E. Kostewicz (2013)

Online Resources

- Choice Boards (Goalbook Toolkit, n.d.a; https://goalbookapp.com/toolkit/v/strategy/choice-boards)

- "How to Make Student Choice Work" (Gehr, 2020; www.edutopia.org/article/how-make-student-choice-work)

- "7 Choice Board Examples for Remote Learning" (Huebner, 2020; https://kodable.com/learn/choice-board-examples-for-remote-learning)

- "Student Reinforcement Survey" (Los Angeles Unified School District, n.d.; https://achieve.lausd.net/cms/lib/CA01000043/Centricity/domain/361/positive%20behavior/tier%20ii/t2%20resources/Student%20Reinforcement%20Survey.pdf)

CHAPTER 3: TOKEN ECONOMIES

The following resources for token economies clarify the importance of this evidence-based practice within the classroom. The textbook and research articles provide details on how to use the token-economy strategy in the classroom with all students, including students who need additional support with their behavior. The online resources provide a how-to and a web-based version of tokens to use in the classroom.

Books

- *Inspiring Kids to Learn: The Token Economy Playbook* by Denise A. Soares, Walter J. Cegelka, and James S. Payne (2015)

Articles

- "A Token Economy Made Easy Through ClassDojo" by Cassie M. Robacker, Christopher J. Rivera, and Sandra H. Warren (2016)

- "A Conceptual Framework for Creating Culturally Responsive Token Economies" by Gess LeBlanc (2016)

- "Practical Components for Getting the Most From a Token Economy" by Kera B. Ackerman, Mark Samudre, and R. Allan Allday (2020)

Online Resources

- ClassDojo (https://classdojo.com)

- "Staying Creative With Token Economies During Behavior Modification" (Steinberg Behavior Solutions, n.d.; https://sbsaba.com/staying-creative-with-token-economies-during-behavior-modification)

- "What Is Tier I Support?" (Center on Positive Behavioral Interventions and Supports, 2022b; www.pbis.org/pbis/tier-1)

CHAPTER 4: HIGH-PROBABILITY SEQUENCING

The following resources for high-probability sequencing amplify the importance of this evidence-based practice within the classroom. The book offers high-probability sequencing as a practical practice to use with your students. The articles depict the use of high-probability sequencing as an important practice within the classroom. The online resources and videos provide examples and various ways to implement high-probability sequencing within the classroom.

Books

- *Building Positive Momentum for Positive Behavior in Young Children: Strategies for Success in School and Beyond* by Lisa Rogers (2018)

Articles

- "Increasing Classroom Compliance: Using a High-Probability Command Sequence With Noncompliant Students" by Michael I. Axelrod and Amber J. Zank (2012)

- "High-Probability Request Sequence: An Effective, Efficient Low-Intensity Strategy to Support Student Success" by Leslie Ann Bross,

Eric Alan Common, Wendy Peia Oakes, Kathleen Lynne Lane,
Holly M. Menzies, and Robin Parks Ennis (2018)

- "Systematic Review of High Probability Requests in K–12 Settings:
  Examining the Evidence Base" by Eric Alan Common, Leslie Ann
  Bross, Wendy Peia Oakes, Emily Dawn Cantwell, Kathleen Lynne
  Lane, and Kathryn Ann Germer (2019)

Online Resources

- "Fundamental Skill Sheet: High-Probability Requests" (Majeika, n.d.;
  https://iris.peabody.vanderbilt.edu/wp-content/uploads/misc_media/fss
  /pdfs/2018/fss_high_p.pdf)
- "High Probability (High-*P*) Request Sequence" (Comprehensive,
  Integrated Three-Tiered Model of Prevention, 2016–2017; https://
  ci3t.org/wp-content/uploads/2016/11/00_HPRS_Introduction.pdf)

Videos

- "Behavior Momentum" (McGill, 2017; https://mediahub.unl.edu
  /media/7943)
- "High-Probability Requests: High School" (IRIS Center, 2019;
  https://iris.peabody.vanderbilt.edu/mcontent/fss/high-probability
  -requests-high-school)

CHAPTER 5: CLASSWIDE PEER TUTORING

The following resources for classwide peer tutoring (CWPT) elaborate on the
importance of this evidence-based practice within the classroom. The research articles provide evidence to support the effectiveness of CWPT and show the academic
benefit of implementing CWPT. The online resources provide examples of how to
implement CWPT and how to share it with families.

Articles

- "Academic Benefits of Peer Tutoring: A Meta-Analytic Review of
  Single-Case Research" by Lisa Bowman-Perrott, Heather Davis,
  Kimberly Vannest, Lauren Williams, Charles Greenwood, and
  Richard Parker (2013)

- "Classwide Peer Tutoring: Practice, Theory, Research, and Personal Narrative" by Larry Maheady and Jaime Gard (2010)
- "A Systematic Review of Peer Tutoring Interventions for Students With Disabilities" by Elizabeth Talbott, Agata Trzaska, and Jaime L. Zurheide (2017)

Online Resources

- The Peer Tutoring Resource Center's (n.d.) resource library (https://peertutoringresource.org/ptrl/program-design-classroom)
- "Classwide Peer Tutoring: Information for Families" (Center for Effective Collaboration and Practice, 2001; https://readingrockets.org/article/classwide-peer-tutoring-information-families)
- "ClassWide Peer Tutoring" (What Works Clearinghouse, 2007; https://ies.ed.gov/ncee/wwc/Docs/InterventionReports/WWC_CWPT_070907.pdf)
- The Juniper Gardens Children's Project website (https://juniper.ku.edu/juniper-research)

CHAPTER 6: SELF-MONITORING

The following resources for self-monitoring illustrate the importance of this evidence-based practice within the classroom. The articles depict the use of self-monitoring and provide step-by-step processes to using this strategy in the classroom. The online resources and books provide examples and various ways to implement self-monitoring within the classroom.

Books

- *How Did You Miss That? A Story About Teaching Self-Monitoring* by Bryan Smith (2019)
- *The Self & Match System: Systematic Use of Self-Monitoring as a Behavioral Intervention* by Jamie S. Salter and Katharine M. Croce (2014)
- *The Behavior Problems Resource Kit: Forms and Procedures for Identification, Measurement, and Intervention* by Michael J. Asher, Steven B. Gordon, Michael C. Selbst, and Mark Cooperberg (2010)

Articles

- "Goal Setting and Self-Monitoring for Students With Disabilities: Practical Tips and Ideas for Teachers" by Suk-Hyang Lee, Susan B. Palmer, and Michael L. Wehmeyer (2009)

- "Increasing On-Task Behavior in the Classroom: Extension of Self-Monitoring Strategies" by Natalie A. Amato-Zech, Kathryn E. Hoff, and Karla J. Doepke (2006)

- "Self-Monitoring of Attention Versus Self-Monitoring of Academic Performance: Effects Among Students With ADHD in the General Education Classroom" by Karen R. Harris, Barbara Danoff Friedlander, Bruce Saddler, Remedios Frizzelle, and Steve Graham (2005)

- "Using an iPod Touch to Teach Social and Self-Management Skills to an Elementary Student With Emotional/Behavioral Disorders" by Erika Blood, Jesse W. Johnson, Lindsey Ridenour, Karen Simmons, and Starline Crouch (2011)

- "Step-by-Step: Teaching Students to Self-Monitor" by Lisa A. Rafferty (2010)

Online Resources

- "Student Reinforcement Survey" (Los Angeles Unified School District, n.d.; https://achieve.lausd.net/cms/lib/CA01000043/Centricity/domain/361/positive%20behavior/tier%20ii/t2%20resources/Student%20Reinforcement%20Survey.pdf)

- "Self-Monitoring" (Goalbook Toolkit, n.d.b; https://goalbookapp.com/toolkit/v/strategy/self-monitoring)

- "How To: Teach Students to Change Behaviors Through Self-Monitoring" (Wright, 2013; https://interventioncentral.org/self_management_self_monitoring)

- "Step 4: Teach Self-Monitoring Procedures" (IRIS Center, 2008; https://iris.peabody.vanderbilt.edu/module/sr/cresource/q2/p04)

- "SOS: Helping Students Become Independent Learners" module (IRIS Center, 2022; https://iris.peabody.vanderbilt.edu/module/sr/#content)

- "Self Monitoring" (PBIS World, n.d.; https://pbisworld.com/tier-3/self-monitoring)

- "4 Ways Kids Use Self-Monitoring to Learn" (Morin, n.d.; https://understood.org/en/learning-thinking-differences/child-learning-disabilities/executive-functioning-issues/4-ways-kids-use-self-monitoring-to-learn)

CHAPTER 7: OPPORTUNITIES TO RESPOND

The following resources for opportunities to respond (OTRs) encapsulate the importance of this evidence-based practice within the classroom. The articles depict the use of OTRs within the classroom through technology, instruction, content areas, and other important ways. The online resources provide examples and various ways to implement OTRs within the classroom.

Articles

- "Using Technology to Increase Opportunities to Respond" by Ashley Rila, Sara Estrapala, and Allison Leigh Bruhn (2019)

- "Opportunities to Respond: A Key Component of Effective Instruction" by Todd Haydon, Ashley S. MacSuga-Gage, Brandi Simonsen, and Renee Hawkins (2012)

- "Agency and Power in Classroom Names and Naming Practices" by Eseta Tualaulelei (2021)

- "Increasing Opportunities to Respond to Intensify Academic and Behavioral Interventions: A Meta-Analysis" by Alyssa M. Van Camp, Joseph H. Wehby, Brittany Lee N. Martin, Jessica R. Wright, and Kevin S. Sutherland (2020)

- "Providing Student Opportunities to Respond in Reading and Mathematics: A Look Across Grade Levels" by Todd Whitney, Justin T. Cooper, and Amy S. Lingo (2015)

Online Resources

- "Providing Multiple Opportunities to Respond" (Kaimuki Middle School, 2018; https://kaimukimiddle.wordpress.com/2018/08/19/opportunities-to-respond)

- "Strategy: Increasing Opportunities to Respond" (The Classroom Check-Up, n.d.b; www.classroomcheckup.org/increasing-opportunities-to-respond)

CHAPTER 8: PRECORRECTION

The following resources for precorrection help emphasize the importance of this evidence-based practice within the classroom. The articles depict the use of precorrection and provide step-by-step processes to using this strategy in the classroom.

The online resources provide examples and various ways to implement precorrection within the classroom.

Articles

- "Characteristics of Effective Classroom Rules: A Review of the Literature" by Peter Alter and Todd Haydon (2017)

- "Precorrection: An Effective, Efficient, Low-Intensity Strategy to Support Student Success" by Robin Parks Ennis, Kathleen Lynne Lane, Holly M. Menzies, and Penney Patterson Owens (2018)

- "Precorrection: Preventing Predictable Problem Behaviors in School Settings" by Lauren L. Evanovich and Laura Kern (2018)

- "The Importance of Precorrective Statements and Behavior-Specific Praise and Strategies to Increase Their Use" by Melissa Stormont and Wendy Reinke (2009)

Online Resources

- The National Center for Pyramid Model Innovations (NCPMI) website (https://challengingbehavior.cbcs.usf.edu)

- "Strategy: Using Precorrection" (The Classroom Check-Up, n.d.c; https://classroomcheckup.org/using-precorrection)

- "Pre-Correction/Prompting: Behavior" (University of Louisville, n.d.; https://louisville.edu/education/abri/primarylevel/prompting/behavior)

- "Precorrection Planning Form" (The Classroom Check-Up, n.d.a; https://app.classroomcheckup.org/api/resources/file/public/Using _Precorrection-Strategy_Tool.pdf)

- "Precorrection: Example Statements" (Comprehensive, Integrated Three-Tiered Model of Prevention, 2015–2016; https://ci3t.org/tier _library/pc/02_PC_Example_Statements.pdf)

References
and Resources

Ackerman, K. B., Samudre, M., & Allday, R. A. (2020). Practical components for getting the most from a token economy. *TEACHING Exceptional Children, 52*(4), 242–249.

Akechi, H., Senju, A., Uibo, H., Kikuchi, Y., Hasegawa, T., & Hietanen, J. K. (2013). Attention to eye contact in the West and East: Autonomic responses and evaluative ratings. *PLOS ONE, 8*(3), e59312.

Al Dera, H. (2022). Cellular and molecular mechanisms underlying autism spectrum disorders and associated comorbidities: A pathophysiological review. *Biomedicine & Pharmacotherapy, 148*, 112688.

Alter, P., & Haydon, T. (2017). Characteristics of effective classroom rules: A review of the literature. *Teacher Education and Special Education, 40*(2), 114–127.

Amato-Zech, N. A., Hoff, K. E., & Doepke, K. J. (2006). Increasing on-task behavior in the classroom: Extension of self-monitoring strategies. *Psychology in the Schools, 43*(2), 211–221.

Anderson, M. (2016). *Learning to choose, choosing to learn: The key to student motivation and achievement.* Alexandria, VA: Association for Supervision and Curriculum Development.

Andrus, S., Jacobs, C., & Kuriloff, P. (2018). Miles to go: The continuing quest for gender equity in the classroom. *Phi Delta Kappan, 100*(2), 46–50.

Asher, M. J., Gordon, S. B., Selbst, M. C., & Cooperberg, M. (2010). *The behavior problems resource kit: Forms and procedures for identification, measurement, and intervention.* Champaign, IL: Research Press.

Ashman, G., & Snow, P. (2019). Oral language competence: How it relates to classroom behavior. *American Educator, 43*(2), 37–41.

Axelrod, M. I., & Zank, A. J. (2012). Increasing classroom compliance: Using a high-probability command sequence with noncompliant students. *Journal of Behavioral Education, 21*(2), 119–133.

Ayvazo, S., & Aljadeff-Abergel, E. (2014). Classwide peer tutoring for elementary and high school students at risk: Listening to students' voices. *Support for Learning, 29*(1), 76–92.

Bennett, S. N., & Fitzwater, C. (2010). Navajo culture. In S. N. Bennett, *Transcultural nursing.* Accessed at http://freebooks.uvu.edu/NURS3400/index.php/about.html on May 31, 2022.

Bettelheim, B. (1967). *The empty fortress: Infantile autism and the birth of the self.* New York: Free Press.

Blood, E., Johnson, J. W., Ridenour, L., Simmons, K., & Crouch, S. (2011). Using an iPod Touch to teach social and self-management skills to an elementary student with emotional/behavioral disorders. *Education and Treatment of Children, 34*(3), 299–321.

Boogren, T. H. (2018). *Take time for you: Self-care action plans for educators.* Bloomington, IN: Solution Tree Press.

Bowman-Perrott, L., Davis, H., Vannest, K., Williams, L., Greenwood, C., & Parker, R. (2013). Academic benefits of peer tutoring: A meta-analytic review of single-case research. *School Psychology Review, 42*(1), 39–55.

Bross, L. A., Common, E. A., Oakes, W. P., Lane, K. L., Menzies, H. M., & Ennis, R. P. (2018). High-probability request sequence: An effective, efficient low-intensity strategy to support student success. *Beyond Behavior, 27*(3), 140–145.

Bruhn, A., McDaniel, S., & Kreigh, C. (2015). Self-monitoring interventions for students with behavior problems: A systematic review of current research. *Behavioral Disorders, 40*(2), 102–121.

Brumariu, L. E., & Kerns, K. A. (2010). Parent-child attachment and internalizing symptoms in childhood and adolescence: A review of empirical findings and future directions. *Development and Psychopathology, 22*(1), 177–203.

Buffum, A., Mattos, M., & Malone, J. (2018). *Taking action: A handbook for RTI at Work.* Bloomington, IN: Solution Tree Press.

Burdick-Will, J. (2018). Neighborhood violence, peer effects, and academic achievement in Chicago. *Sociology of Education, 91*(3), 205–223.

Carney, S. M. (2021). *The student voice: Experiences of first-generation adult, Latino male tutees learning within a peer tutoring environment.* Doctoral dissertation, Brandman University. Accessed at https://digitalcommons.umassglobal.edu/edd_dissertations/399 on August 20, 2022.

Center for Effective Collaboration and Practice. (2001). *Classwide peer tutoring: Information for families.* Accessed at https://readingrockets.org/article/classwide-peer-tutoring-information-families on April 5, 2022.

Center on Positive Behavioral Interventions and Supports. (2022a). *Getting started with PBIS.* Accessed at www.pbis.org/pbis/getting-started on May 3, 2022.

Center on Positive Behavioral Interventions and Supports. (2022b). *What is tier 1 support?* Accessed at www.pbis.org/pbis/tier-1 on May 5, 2022.

Center on Positive Behavioral Interventions and Supports. (2022c). *What is tier 2 support?* Accessed at www.pbis.org/pbis/tier-2 on May 5, 2022.

Center on Positive Behavioral Interventions and Supports. (2022d). *What is tier 3 support?* Accessed at www.pbis.org/pbis/tier-3 on May 5, 2022.

Cho, B. E. (2004). Issues concerning Korean learners of English: English education in Korea and some common difficulties of Korean students. *The East Asian Learner, 1*(2), 31–36.

Council for Exceptional Children. (1987). *Academy for effective instruction: Working with mildly handicapped students.* Reston, VA: Author.

The Classroom Check-Up. (n.d.a). *Precorrection planning form.* Accessed at https://app
.classroomcheckup.org/api/resources/file/public/Using_Precorrection-Strategy_Tool.pdf on
April 5, 2022.

The Classroom Check-Up. (n.d.b). *Strategy: Increasing opportunities to respond.* Accessed at www
.classroomcheckup.org/increasing-opportunities-to-respond on April 5, 2022.

The Classroom Check-Up. (n.d.c). *Strategy: Using precorrection.* Accessed at https://classroomcheckup
.org/using-precorrection on April 5, 2022.

Colker, R. (2015). Blaming mothers: A disability perspective. *Boston University Law Review, 95*(3),
1205–1224.

Colvin, G., Sugai, G., & Patching, B. (1993). Precorrection: An instructional approach for managing
predictable problem behaviors. *Intervention in School and Clinic, 28*(3), 143–150.

Common, E. A., Bross, L. A., Oakes, W. P., Cantwell, E. D., Lane, K. L., & Germer, K. A. (2019).
Systematic review of high probability requests in K–12 settings: Examining the evidence base.
Behavioral Disorders, 45(1), 3–21.

Comprehensive, Integrated Three-Tiered Model of Prevention. (2015–2016). *Precorrection: Example
statements.* Accessed at https://ci3t.org/tier_library/pc/02_PC_Example_Statements.pdf on
April 5, 2022.

Comprehensive, Integrated Three-Tiered Model of Prevention. (2016–2017). *High probability (high-p)
request sequence.* Accessed at https://ci3t.org/wp-content/uploads/2016/11/00_HPRS
_Introduction.pdf on April 5, 2022.

Davis, M. (2014). Stop the blame game: Teachers and parents working together to improve outcomes for
students with behavior disorders. *Journal of the American Academy of Special Education Professionals*,
48–59. Accessed at https://files.eric.ed.gov/fulltext/EJ1134852.pdf on January 31, 2022.

Davis, T. N., Dacus, S., Bankhead, J., Haupert, M., Fuentes, L., Zoch, T., et al. (2014). A comparison
of self-monitoring with and without reinforcement to improve on-task classroom behavior. *Journal
of School Counseling, 12*(12), 1–23.

Delgado-Gaitan, C. (1992). School matters in the Mexican-American home: Socializing children to
education. *American Educational Research Journal, 29*(3), 495–513.

Edwards, S. (2011). Developing diversity dispositions for White culturally responsive teachers. *Action in
Teacher Education, 33*(5–6), 493–508.

Edwards, S., & Edick, N. A. (2013). Culturally responsive teaching for significant relationships. *Journal
of Praxis in Multicultural Education, 7*(1), 1–19.

Elkins, K., & Nudelman, M. (2015). *The shocking differences in basic body language around the
world.* Accessed at www.businessinsider.com/body-language-around-the-world-2015-3 on
August 5, 2022.

Emerson, E. (1995). *Challenging behaviour: Analysis and intervention in people with learning disabilities.*
Cambridge, MA: Cambridge University Press.

Ennis, R. P., Lane, K. L., Menzies, H. M., & Owens, P. P. (2018). Precorrection: An effective, efficient,
low-intensity strategy to support student success. *Beyond Behavior, 27*(3), 146–152.

Ennis, R. P., Royer, D. J., Lane, K. L., & Griffith, C. E. (2017). A systematic review of precorrection in
PK–12 settings. *Education and Treatment of Children, 40*(4), 465–496.

Evanovich, L. L., & Kern, L. (2018). Precorrection: Preventing predictable problem behaviors in school
settings. *Beyond Behavior, 27*(2), 90–98.

Evans, G. W., & Rosenbaum, J. (2008). Self-regulation and the income-achievement gap. *Early
Childhood Research Quarterly, 23*(4), 504–514.

Farley, C., Torres, C., Wailehua, C. T., & Cook, L. (2012). Evidence-based practices for students with emotional and behavioral disorders: Improving academic achievement. *Beyond Behavior*, *21*(2), 37–43.

Farmer, T. W., Reinke, W. M., & Brooks, D. S. (2014). Managing classrooms and challenging behavior: Theoretical considerations and critical issues. *Journal of Emotional and Behavioral Disorders*, *22*(2), 67–73.

Filippello, P., Larcan, R., Sorrenti, L., Buzzai, C., Orecchio, S., & Costa, S. (2017). The mediating role of maladaptive perfectionism in the association between psychological control and learned helplessness. *Improving Schools*, *20*(2), 113–126.

Fuchs, L. S., Fuchs, D., & Compton, D. L. (2010). Rethinking response to intervention at middle school and high school. *School Psychology Review*, *39*(1), 22–28.

Fullam, J. P. (2017). From seeing to believing: Using instructional video to develop culturally responsive teaching. *Journal for Multicultural Education*, *11*(2), 131–148.

Gaias, L. M., Johnson, S. L., Bottiani, J. H., Debnam, K. J., & Bradshaw, C. P. (2019). Examining teachers' classroom management profiles: Incorporating a focus on culturally responsive practice. *Journal of School Psychology*, *76*(2), 124–139.

Garwood, J. D., Van Loan, C. L., & Werts, M. G. (2017). Mindset of paraprofessionals serving students with emotional and behavioral disorders. *Intervention in School and Clinic*, *53*(4), 206–211.

Garibay, J. C. (2015). *Creating a positive classroom climate for diversity*. Los Angeles: UCLA Diversity and Faculty Development.

Gay, G. (2018). *Culturally responsive teaching: Theory, research, and practice* (3rd ed.). New York: Teachers College Press.

Gehr, L. (2020, February 11). How to make student choice work. *Edutopia*. Accessed at www.edutopia.org/article/how-make-student-choice-work on February 1, 2022.

Ghasemi, F. (2021). A motivational response to the inefficiency of teachers' practices towards students with learned helplessness. *Learning and Motivation*, *73*, 101705.

Gladden, R. M., Vivolo-Kantor, A. M., Hamburger, M. E., & Lumpkin, C. D. (2014). *Bullying surveillance among youths: Uniform definitions for public health and recommended data elements* (Version 1.0). Atlanta, GA: National Center for Injury Prevention and Control. Accessed at https://cdc.gov/violenceprevention/pdf/bullying-definitions-final-a.pdf on February 1, 2022.

Goalbook Toolkit. (n.d.a). *Choice boards*. Accessed at https://goalbookapp.com/toolkit/v/strategy/choice-boards on April 5, 2022.

Goalbook Toolkit. (n.d.b). *Self-monitoring*. Accessed at https://goalbookapp.com/toolkit/v/strategy/self-monitoring on April 5, 2022.

Gorski, P. C. (2018). *Reaching and teaching students in poverty: Strategies for erasing the opportunity gap* (2nd ed.). New York: Teachers College Press.

Gregory, A., & Roberts, G. (2017). Teacher beliefs and the overrepresentation of Black students in classroom discipline. *Theory Into Practice*, *56*(3), 187–194.

Grothe, T. (2020). Exploring intercultural communication. *LibreTexts*. Accessed at https://socialsci.libretexts.org/Courses/Butte_College/Exploring_Intercultural_Communication_(Grothe) on January 31, 2022.

Gwernan-Jones, R., Moore, D. A., Garside, R., Richardson, M., Thompson-Coon, J., Rogers, M., et al. (2015). ADHD, parent perspectives and parent–teacher relationships: Grounds for conflict. *British Journal of Special Education*, *42*(3), 279–300.

Hallahan, D. P., Kauffman, J. M., & Pullen, P. C. (2019). *Exceptional learners: An introduction to special education* (14th ed.). New York: Pearson.

Harris, K. R., Friedlander, B. D., Saddler, B., Frizzelle, R., & Graham, S. (2005). Self-monitoring of attention versus self-monitoring of academic performance: Effects among students with ADHD in the general education classroom. *Journal of Special Education, 39*(3), 145–156.

Haydon, T., MacSuga-Gage, A. S., Simonsen, B., & Hawkins, R. (2012). Opportunities to respond: A key component of effective instruction. *Beyond Behavior, 22*(1), 23–31.

Herbel-Eisenmann, B., & Shah, N. (2019). Detecting and reducing bias in questioning patterns. *Mathematics Teaching in the Middle School, 24*(5), 282–289.

Hinshaw, S. P. (1992). Externalizing behavior problems and academic underachievement in childhood and adolescence: Causal relationships and underlying mechanisms. *Psychological Bulletin, 111*(1), 127–155.

Horner, R. H., & Sugai, G. (2015). School-wide PBIS: An example of applied behavior analysis implemented at a scale of social importance. *Behavior Analysis in Practice, 8*(1), 80–85.

Huebner, G. (2020, August 3). *7 choice board examples for remote learning* [Blog post]. Accessed at https://kodable.com/learn/choice-board-examples-for-remote-learning on February 1, 2022.

Hwa-Froelich, D. A. (Ed.). (2015). *Social communication development and disorders.* New York: Psychology Press.

Individuals With Disabilities Education Improvement Act of 2004, Pub. L. No. 108-446 § 300.115 (2004).

IRIS Center. (2008). Step 4: Teach self-monitoring procedures. In *SOS: Helping students become independent learners* [Module]. Accessed at https://iris.peabody.vanderbilt.edu/module/sr/cresource /q2/p04 on June 9, 2022.

IRIS Center. (2019, April 18). *High-probability requests: High school* [Video file]. Accessed at https:// iris.peabody.vanderbilt.edu/mcontent/fss/high-probability-requests-high-school on April 5, 2022.

IRIS Center. (2022). *SOS: Helping students become independent learners* [Module]. Accessed at https:// iris.peabody.vanderbilt.edu/module/sr/#content on April 5, 2022.

Ivy, J. W., Meindl, J. N., Overley, E., & Robson, K. M. (2017). Token economy: A systematic review of procedural descriptions. *Behavior Modification, 41*(5), 708–737.

Jensen, E. (2009). *Teaching with poverty in mind: What being poor does to kids' brains and what schools can do about it.* Alexandria, VA: Association for Supervision and Curriculum Development.

Jensen, M., Chassin, L., & Gonzales, N. A. (2017). Neighborhood moderation of sensation seeking effects on adolescent substance use initiation. *Journal of Youth and Adolescence, 46*(9), 1953–1967.

Joffe, V. L., & Black, E. (2012). Social, emotional, and behavioral functioning of secondary school students with low academic and language performance: Perspectives from students, teachers, and parents. *Language, Speech, and Hearing Services in Schools, 43*(4), 461–473.

Johnson, L., & Larwin, K. H. (2020). Systemic bias in public education: The exception of African American males enrolled in gifted and Advanced Placement courses. *Journal of Organizational and Educational Leadership, 6*(2). Accessed at https://digitalcommons.gardner-webb.edu/joel/vol6/iss2/3 on January 31, 2022.

Jolivette, K., Ennis, R. P., & Swoszowski, N. C. (2017). Educator "what-ifs": The feasibility of choice making in the classroom. *Beyond Behavior, 26*(2), 74–80.

Kaimuki Middle School. (2018, August 19). *Providing multiple opportunities to respond* [Blog post]. Accessed at https://kaimukimiddle.wordpress.com/2018/08/19/opportunities-to-respond on April 5, 2022.

Kalbfleisch, P. J. (2009). Effective health communication in Native populations in North America. *Journal of Language and Social Psychology, 28*(2), 158–173.

Kanner, L. (1943). Autistic disturbances of affective contact. *Nervous Child, 2*(3), 217–250.

Kauffman, J. M., & Landrum, T. J. (2018). *Characteristics of emotional and behavioral disorders of children and youth* (11th ed.). New York: Pearson.

Kieran, L., & Anderson, C. (2019). Connecting universal design for learning with culturally responsive teaching. *Education and Urban Society, 51*(9), 1202–1216.

King, S. A., & Kostewicz, D. E. (2014). Choice-based stimulus preference assessment for children with or at-risk for emotional disturbance in educational settings. *Education and Treatment of Children, 37*(3), 531–558.

Knowles, C., Meng, P., & Machalicek, W. (2015). Task sequencing for students with emotional and behavioral disorders: A systematic review. *Behavior Modification, 39*(1), 136–166.

Kremer, K. P., Flower, A., Huang, J., & Vaughn, M. G. (2016). Behavior problems and children's academic achievement: A test of growth-curve models with gender and racial differences. *Children and Youth Services Review, 67*(C), 95–104.

Kroeper, K. M., Fried, A. C., & Murphy, M. C. (2022). Towards fostering growth mindset classrooms: Identifying teaching behaviors that signal instructors' fixed and growth mindsets beliefs to students. *Social Psychology of Education,* 1–28.

Landrum, T. J., & Sweigart, C. A. (2014). Simple, evidence-based interventions for classic problems of emotional and behavioral disorders. *Beyond Behavior, 23*(3), 3–9.

Larson, K. E., Pas, E. T., Bradshaw, C. P., Rosenberg, M. S., & Day-Vines, N. L. (2018). Examining how proactive management and culturally responsive teaching relate to student behavior: Implications for measurement and practice. *School Psychology Review, 47*(2), 153–166.

Leath, S., Mathews, C., Harrison, A., & Chavous, T. (2019). Racial identity, racial discrimination, and classroom engagement outcomes among Black girls and boys in predominantly Black and predominantly White school districts. *American Educational Research Journal, 56*(4), 1318–1352.

LeBlanc, G. (2016). A conceptual framework for creating culturally responsive token economies. *Curriculum and Teaching, 31*(1), 27–45.

Lee, R. E. (2018). Breaking down barriers and building bridges: Transformative practices in community- and school-based urban teacher preparation. *Journal of Teacher Education, 69*(2), 118–126.

Lee, S.-H., Palmer, S. B., & Wehmeyer, M. L. (2009). Goal setting and self-monitoring for students with disabilities: Practical tips and ideas for teachers. *Intervention in School and Clinic, 44*(3), 139–145.

Lewis, R. D. (2006). *When cultures collide: Leading across cultures* (3rd ed.). Boston: Brealey.

Lewis, R. D. (2018). *When cultures collide: Leading across cultures* (4th ed.). Boston: Brealey.

Lewis, T. J., & Sugai, G. (1999). Effective behavior support: A systems approach to proactive schoolwide management. *Focus on Exceptional Children, 31*(6), 1–24.

Los Angeles Unified School District. (n.d.). *Student reinforcement survey.* (n.d.). Accessed at https://achieve.lausd.net/cms/lib/CA01000043/Centricity/domain/361/positive%20behavior/tier%20ii/t2%20resources/Student%20Reinforcement%20Survey.pdf on February 1, 2022.

Luthar, S. S., Barkin, S. H., & Crossman, E. J. (2013). "I can, therefore I must": Fragility in the upper-middle classes. *Development and Psychopathology, 25*(4, part 2), 1529–1549.

MacSuga-Gage, A. S., & Simonsen, B. (2015). Examining the effects of teacher-directed opportunities to respond on student outcomes: A systematic review of the literature. *Education and Treatment of Children, 38*(2), 211–239.

Maheady, L., & Gard, J. (2010). Classwide peer tutoring: Practice, theory, research, and personal narrative. *Intervention in School and Clinic, 46*(2), 71–78.

Majeika, C. (n.d.). *Fundamental skill sheet: High-probability requests.* Accessed at https://iris.peabody .vanderbilt.edu/wp-content/uploads/misc_media/fss/pdfs/2018/fss_high_p.pdf on April 5, 2022.

Marrun, N. A. (2018). Culturally responsive teaching across PK–20: Honoring the historical naming practices of students of color. *Taboo: The Journal of Culture and Education, 17*(3), 6–25.

McCormick, R. (2017). Does access to green space impact the mental well-being of children: A systematic review. *Journal of Pediatric Nursing, 37,* 3–7.

McDougall, D., Morrison, C., & Awana, B. (2012). Students with disabilities use tactile cued self-monitoring to improve academic productivity during independent tasks. *Journal of Instructional Psychology, 39*(2), 119–130.

McGill, T. (2017, June 26). *Behavior momentum* [Video file]. Accessed at https://mediahub.unl.edu /media/7943 on April 5, 2022.

Milner, H. R., IV, Cunningham, H. B., Delale-O'Connor, L., & Kestenberg, E. G. (2019). *"These kids are out of control": Why we must reimagine "classroom management" for equity.* Thousand Oaks, CA: Corwin Press.

Milner, H. R., IV, Cunningham, H. B., Murray, I. E., & Alvarez, A. (2017). Supporting students living below the poverty line. *National Youth Advocacy and Resilience Journal, 2*(2), 51–68.

Morin, A. (n.d.). *4 ways kids use self-monitoring to learn.* Accessed at https://understood.org/en/learning -thinking-differences/child-learning-disabilities/executive-functioning-issues/4-ways-kids-use-self -monitoring-to-learn on April 5, 2022.

National Center for Education Statistics. (2020). Racial/ethnic enrollment in public schools. *Condition of Education.* Washington, DC: Institute of Education Sciences. Accessed at https://nces.ed.gov /programs/coe/indicator_cge.asp#:~:text=In%20fall%202017%2C%20of%20the,million%20were %20American%20Indian%2FAlaska on February 1, 2022.

No Child Left Behind (NCLB) Act of 2001, Pub. L. No. 107-110, § 115, Stat. 1425 (2002).

Obiakor, F. E., Bakken, J. P., Simpson, C., & Algozzine, B. (2010). Culturally responsive teaching. In B. Algozzine, A. P. Daunic, & S. W. Smith (Eds.), *Preventing problem behaviors: Schoolwide programs and classroom practices* (2nd ed., pp. 181–194). Thousand Oaks, CA: Corwin Press.

Orkin, M., May, S., & Wolf, M. (2017). How parental support during homework contributes to helpless behaviors among struggling readers. *Reading Psychology, 38*(5), 506–541.

Ozer, E. J., Lavi, I., Douglas, L., & Wolf, J. P. (2017). Protective factors for youth exposed to violence in their communities: A review of family, school, and community moderators. *Journal of Clinical Child and Adolescent Psychology, 46*(3), 353–378.

Parks, M. (2017). Simple strategies to develop rapport with students and build a positive classroom climate. *The National Teaching & Learning Forum, 26*(5), 4–6.

Patall, E. A., Cooper, H., & Wynn, S. R. (2010). The effectiveness and relative importance of choice in the classroom. *Journal of Educational Psychology, 102*(4), 896–915.

PBIS World. (n.d.). *Self monitoring.* Accessed at https://pbisworld.com/tier-3/self-monitoring on April 5, 2022.

Peer Tutoring Resource Center. (n.d.). *Resource library.* Accessed at https://peertutoringresource.org /ptrl/program-design-classroom on April 5, 2022.

Pinker, S. (2004). Why nature and nurture won't go away. *Daedalus, 133*(4), 5–17.

Quan, Y. Y. (2015, August). Analysis of silence in intercultural communication. In *2015 International Conference on Economy, Management and Education Technology* (pp. 155–159). Amsterdam, North Holland, the Netherlands: Atlantis Press.

Rafferty, L. A. (2010). Step-by-step: Teaching students to self-monitor. *TEACHING Exceptional Children, 43*(2), 50–58.

Rila, A., Estrapala, S., & Bruhn, A. L. (2019). Using technology to increase opportunities to respond. *Beyond Behavior, 28*(1), 36–45.

Robacker, C. M., Rivera, C. J., & Warren, S. H. (2016). A token economy made easy through ClassDojo. *Intervention in School and Clinic, 52*(1), 39–43.

Rogers, L. (2018). *Building positive momentum for positive behavior in young children: Strategies for success in school and beyond.* Philadelphia: Kingsley.

Romm, K. F., Barry, C. M., & Alvis, L. M. (2020). How the rich get riskier: Parenting and higher-SES emerging adults' risk behaviors. *Journal of Adult Development, 27*(5), 281–293.

Royer, D. J., Lane, K. L., Cantwell, E. D., & Messenger, M. L. (2017). A systematic review of the evidence base for instructional choice in K–12 settings. *Behavioral Disorders, 42*(3), 89–107.

RTI Action Network. (n.d.). *What is RTI?* Accessed at www.rtinetwork.org/learn/what/whatisrti on June 26, 2022.

Rugsaken, K. (2006). *Body speaks: Body language around the world.* Accessed at https://nacada.ksu.edu /Resources/Clearinghouse/View-Articles/Body-Language-Around-the-World.aspx on June 9, 2022.

Salter, J. S., & Croce, K. M. (2014). *The self & match system: Systematic use of self-monitoring as a behavioral intervention.* San Marcos, CA: Self & Match Educational Consultation.

Sanders, C., & DeBlois, D. (Directors). (2002). *Lilo & Stitch.* United States: Walt Disney Feature Animation.

Scheuermann, B. K., & Hall, J. A. (2016). *Positive behavioral supports for the classroom* (3rd ed.). Boston: Pearson.

Scott, T. M. (2017). *Teaching behavior: Managing classrooms through effective instruction.* Thousand Oaks, CA: Corwin Press.

Scott, T. M., Alter, P. J., & Hirn, R. G. (2011). An examination of typical classroom context and instruction for students with and without behavioral disorders. *Education and Treatment of Children, 34*(4), 619–641.

Sektnan, M., McClelland, M. M., Acock, A., & Morrison, F. J. (2010). Relations between early family risk, children's behavioral regulation, and academic achievement. *Early Children Research Quarterly, 25*(4), 464–479.

Seward, M. (2019, April 11). *Decolonizing the classroom: Step 1* [Blog post]. Accessed at https://ncte.org /blog/2019/04/decolonizing-the-classroom on January 31, 2022.

Skerbetz, M. D., & Kostewicz, D. E. (2013). Academic choice for included students with emotional and behavioral disorders. *Preventing School Failure: Alternative Education for Children and Youth, 57*(4), 212–222.

Skiba, R. J., Albrecht, S., & Losen, D. (2013). CCBD's position summary on federal policy on disproportionality in special education. *Behavioral Disorders, 38*(2), 108–120.

Skiba, R. J., Horner, R. H., Chung, C.-G., Rausch, M. K., May, S. L., & Tobin, T. (2011). Race is not neutral: A national investigation of African American and Latino disproportionality in school discipline. *School Psychology Review, 40*(1), 85–107.

Smith, A. (n.d.). *Building (and maintaining) rapport in the classroom.* Accessed at www.depts.ttu.edu /tlpdc/Resources/Teaching_resources/TLPDC_teaching_resources/Documents/Building _Rapport_new.pdf on June 7, 2022.

Smith, B. (2019). *How did you miss that? A story about teaching self-monitoring.* Boys Town, NE: Boys Town Press.

Soares, D. A., Cegelka, W. J., & Payne, J. S. (2015). *Inspiring kids to learn: The token economy playbook.* San Diego, CA: Cognella Academic.

Steinberg Behavior Solutions. (n.d.). *Staying creative with token economies during behavior modification.* Accessed at https://sbsaba.com/staying-creative-with-token-economies-during-behavior-modification on April 5, 2022.

Stiles, J. (2011). Brain development and the nature versus nurture debate. *Progress in Brain Research, 189,* 3–22.

Stormont, M., & Reinke, W. (2009). The importance of precorrective statements and behavior-specific praise and strategies to increase their use. *Beyond Behavior, 18*(3), 26–32.

Tabery, J. (2014). *Beyond versus: The struggle to understand the interaction of nature and nurture.* Cambridge, MA: MIT Press.

Taie, S., & Goldring, R. (2020). *Characteristics of public and private elementary and secondary school teachers in the United States: Results from the 2017–18 National Teacher and Principal Survey—First look* (NCES 2020-142). Washington, DC: National Center for Education Statistics.

Talbott, E., Trzaska, A., & Zurheide, J. L. (2017). A systematic review of peer tutoring interventions for students with disabilities. In M. T. Hughes & E. Talbott (Eds.), *The Wiley handbook of diversity in special education* (pp. 321–356). Malden, MA: Wiley.

Tualaulelei, E. (2021). Agency and power in classroom names and naming practices. *Ethnography and Education, 16*(1), 18–30.

University of Louisville. (n.d.). *Pre-correction/prompting: Behavior.* Accessed at https://louisville.edu/education/abri/primarylevel/prompting/behavior on April 5, 2022.

Valdés, G. (1996). *Con respeto: Bridging the distances between culturally diverse families and schools—An ethnographic portrait.* New York: Teachers College Press.

Van Camp, A. M., Wehby, J. H., Martin, B. L. N., Wright, J. R., & Sutherland, K. S. (2020). Increasing opportunities to respond to intensify academic and behavioral interventions: A meta-analysis. *School Psychology Review, 49*(1), 31–46.

Watson, F. F., Bishop, M. C., & Ferdinand-James, D. (2017). Instructional strategies to help online students learn: Feedback from online students. *TechTrends, 61*(5), 420–427.

Webber, J., Anderson, T., & Otey, L. (1991). Teacher mindsets for surviving in BD classrooms. *Intervention in School and Clinic, 26*(5), 288–292.

What Works Clearinghouse. (2007). *ClassWide Peer Tutoring* (WWC Intervention Report). Washington, DC: Institute of Education Sciences. Accessed at https://ies.ed.gov/ncee/wwc/Docs/InterventionReports/WWC_CWPT_070907.pdf on April 5, 2022.

White, R., & Renk, K. (2012). Externalizing behavior problems during adolescence: An ecological perspective. *Journal of Child and Family Studies, 21*(1), 158–171.

Whitney, T., Cooper, J. T., & Lingo, A. S. (2015). Providing student opportunities to respond in reading and mathematics: A look across grade levels. *Preventing School Failure: Alternative Education for Children and Youth, 59*(1), 14–21.

Wills, H. P., Caldarella, P., Mason, B. A., Lappin, A., & Anderson, D. H. (2019). Improving student behavior in middle schools: Results of a classroom management intervention. *Journal of Positive Behavior Interventions, 21*(4), 213–227.

Wink, M. N., LaRusso, M. D., & Smith, R. L. (2021). Teacher empathy and students with problem behaviors: Examining teachers' perceptions, responses, relationships, and burnout. *Psychology in the Schools, 58*(8), 1575–1596.

Wolpert-Gawron, H. (2018). *Just ask us: Kids speak out on student engagement.* Thousand Oaks, CA: Corwin Press.

Wong, H. K., & Wong, R. T. (2018). *The first days of school: How to be an effective teacher* (5th ed.). Mountain View, CA: Wong.

Wood, C. L., Kisinger, K. W., Brosh, C. R., Fisher, L. B., & Muharib, R. (2018). Stopping behavior before it starts: Antecedent interventions for challenging behavior. *TEACHING Exceptional Children, 50*(6), 356–363.

Wright, J. (2013). *How to: Teach students to change behaviors through self-monitoring.* Accessed at https://interventioncentral.org/self_management_self_monitoring on April 5, 2022.

Wright, J. (2017, October 24). *Finding the spark: Teacher communication tools to battle learned helplessness and engage the unmotivated student* [Conference presentation]. Presented at the Response to Intervention Best Practices Institute workshop, Wrightsville Beach, NC.

Xu, D., Solanki, S., & Fink, J. (2021). College acceleration for all? Mapping racial gaps in Advanced Placement and dual enrollment participation. *American Educational Research Journal, 58*(5), 954–992.

Yama, H., & Zakaria, N. (2019). Explanations for cultural differences in thinking: Easterners' dialectical thinking and Westerners' linear thinking. *Journal of Cognitive Psychology, 31*(4), 487–506.

Yeager, D. S., & Dweck, C. S. (2020). What can be learned from growth mindset controversies? *American Psychologist, 75*(9), 1269–1284.

Yell, M. L., Meadows, N. B., Drasgow, E., & Shriner, J. G. (2013). *Evidence-based practices for educating students with emotional and behavioral disorders* (2nd ed.). Boston: Pearson.

Zaheer, I., Maggin, D., McDaniel, S., McIntosh, K., Rodriguez, B. J., & Fogt, J. B. (2019). Implementation of promising practices that support students with emotional and behavioral disorders. *Behavioral Disorders, 44*(2), 117–128.

Index

F

families

blame game and, 21–24

community and, 9

culture and, 30

five steps to positive parent-teacher collaboration, 22

high-probability sequencing and, 78

nurture and, 7–8

refrigerator mothers, 20

strategies for developing significant relationships with students and, 42

token-economy systems and, 63–64

feedback

classwide peer tutoring and, 90, 92, 96, 99

high-probability requests and, 77, 78–79

opportunities to respond and, 130, 131

precorrection and, 147

research on, 137

token economies and, 57, 61

fixed mindset, 19. *See also* growth mindset

following directions and precorrection, 147

G

genetics, 15–16

goals

opportunities to respond and, 133, 134

self-monitoring and, 113–114

growth mindset, 24, 26

H

high-probability requests

definition of, 76

example tasks for high- and low-probability requests, 84

high-probability sequencing

about, 75–76

concluding thoughts, 86

cultural and linguistic diversity and, 77, 81–82

data collection and, 77, 78, 80–81

delivery of and reinforcements for, 77, 79–80

dos and don'ts for, 86

examples of how to utilize, 83–86

how to implement, 76–83

reinforcements, identifying, 77, 78–79

reproducibles for, 87–88

resources for teachers for, 168–169

scenarios for, 75, 80, 84, 85

student interests and, 77–78, 82–83

hypervigilance, 9

I

IEP meetings/teams, 82, 109, 110

implementation of strategies, 163

independent work

choice and, 40–41, 46, 47

classwide peer tutoring and, 91

precorrection and, 146

scenarios with, 35, 40, 45, 50, 123, 129

individual token-economy systems. *See also* token economies

about, 59–60

benefits of, 61

fading the tokens, 67

scenario for, 67

individualistic societies, 82

Individuals With Disabilities Education Improvement Act (IDEA), 21

instruction and promoting student success, 150

interdependent societies, 82

interest inventories, 82–83. *See also* student interests

internalizing behaviors, 8. *See also* behavior

Motivating Students Who Don't Care, Second Edition
Allen N. Mendler
In the second edition of this valuable resource, Allen Mendler offers specific, practical strategies on how to reignite enthusiasm in even the most unmotivated students. Learn classroom and behavior management strategies that will help support struggling students and build positive teacher-student relationships.
BKF970

The Tactical Teacher
Dale Ripley
Positively influence the behavior of even your most challenging students. In *The Tactical Teacher*, author Dale Ripley shares a plethora of tactics, ranging from persuasive dialogue to environmental details, proven to improve classroom behavior and increase student learning.
BKG025

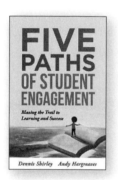

Five Paths of Student Engagement
Dennis Shirley and Andy Hargreaves
This is a breakthrough book on student engagement. Join Dennis Shirley and Andy Hargreaves, two award-winning authors and leaders in their field, on a profound educational quest that will take you through exciting and challenging terrain. *Five Paths of Student Engagement* will open your eyes, heart, and mind and empower you to implement practices that lead directly to your students' well-being, learning, and success.
BKF707

The Wraparound Guide
Leigh Colburn and Linda Beggs
With this timely guide, you will discover actionable steps for launching and sustaining wraparound services embedded within your school that support the whole child. Amplify student voice and build mental health with strategies that improve academic achievement and classroom behavior.
BKF956

Solution Tree | Press

a division of
Solution Tree

Visit SolutionTree.com or call 800.733.6786 to order.